The Art and Science of Self Publishing

Simple Guide to Self Publishing World Class Books

Doug Purcell

Purcell consult

E-book ISBN: 978-0-9973262-3-9
Paperback ISBN: 978-0-9973262-4-6
Purcell Consult http://www.purcellconsult.com

Titles from Purcell Consult are available at discount when purchased in bulk for gifts, corporate events, or premiums. Send email to purcellconsult@gmail.com with inquiry. Responses are typically given within 1-2 business days.

CONTENTS

CHAPTER III:
The Birth of a Book

CHAPTER IV:
E-book distribution & Print on Demand

CHAPTER V:
Tactical Amazon Promotion

CHAPTER VI:
Raging Reviews

CHAPTER VII:
Event Hosting

Intro

Self-publishing your own book is more accessible to you now than in any other time in history. You have a mega-billion-dollar behemoth in Amazon, empowering authors globally to broadcast their creative works. You also have quick access to countless of print-on-demand (POD) services such as CreateSpace (Amazon) and Lightning Source (Ingram) that allow authors to convert their digital content into high-quality paperbacks or hardcovers.

Creating high-quality books is important for customer growth and enduring credibility. A stigma is attached to self-published books as opposed to ones produced by traditional publishing companies, such as: HarperCollins, Penguin Random House, and Simon & Schuster. Most self-published books are produced by a one-man-army while those produced through traditional publishing companies are backed by multi-million dollar corporations. These companies have decades worth of experience in the art of creating world-class books. It's difficult for someone with little to no experience to make noise self-publishing without the proper knowledge. That's why I'm a huge fan of knowledge-sharing. The more you know, the better chance you have in succeeding with your self-publishing enterprise. This is exactly where this book comes in handy.

I personally believe that writing a book is one of the finest low-risk investments an average person can make in their career. There are so many added benefits, such as an extra layer of credibility, dramatically enhancing your professional skills, and adding an extra stream of income to your bottom-line.

When a professional writes a book based on the experiences in their field, they help elevate their credibility and foster their professional branding. This can kick-start lucrative career opportunities, such as workshop presentations, speaking gigs, or consulting.

When you self-publish your own book, you become a hybrid writer and publisher. This requires an array of skills. Not only do you take part in writing, editing, and proofreading your book, but you also participate in market research, project management, marketing, sales, event management, and web design. Many of these skills are easily transferable to a wide-spectrum of industries so producing a high-quality book deepens your skills as a professional.

When an author receives payment for their intellectual property, it's known as royalties. Having your own high quality, well-received, and well-promoted book is akin to having an asset. It will generate money for you and you can also find creative ways to profit from it. Through the power of self-publishing, authors are no longer disenfranchised when a large publisher rejects their manuscript. Instead, they now have the tools and resources to convert their brainchild into reality.

The methods taught in this book provide knowledge you'll need to research, plan, write, produce, publish, and promote your very own book. It is your one-stop-shop for everything self-publishing. However, not even an online encyclopedia can provide information about everything under the sun. Therefore, various links have been incorporated into this guide as resources for further study.

If you're new to self-publishing, then you have a fun adventure ahead of you. Make sure to actively read this book by taking notes, highlighting, and reviewing sections you need more clarity on. Once that's done, the final step is to go out and start executing your plan. It's easy to start writing; it's harder to finish a book. But the real test is taking a final manuscript and putting it into publication. That's the ultimate challenge you need to meet to officially etch your name as a published author. This book will help you reach that destination of your journey one chapter at a time.

CHAPTER I:
How to carve out a niche

Before you open your word processor and get typing, wait just one minute. Something I will say multiple times throughout this book is that once you decide to become a self-publisher, you're not only a content creator, you're also entering the business of books. Therefore, instead of jumping head-first into the exciting world of writing, I would recommend conducting extensive market research to see if there's demand for what you want to write about. Like the way a coach scouts a rival team, you should carefully analyze how competitive your prospective genre is, the average price of books, and the strengths and weaknesses of your competition. This chapter will equip you with beneficial resources you can use to get ideas for what to write about and how to test the concept of your book before it goes live on the market.

Amazon

When it comes to finding credible market research data for books, it's very difficult to beat out Amazon. After all, it's the world's number one online retailer for books, an absolute mecca for book lovers from every corner of the planet. You can get invaluable sales-driven data, such as insights about the bestselling books, movers and shakers, and most wished for books. To discover the top-selling books on Amazon, *visit Amazon Best Sellers* in Books.[1] Amazon provides lists about bestselling books broken down by categories. For example, you can analyze the bestseller list for Arts & Photography,[2] Business & Money,[3] and Humor & Entertainment,[4] to name a

---

few. All these lists are updated hourly. By analyzing the books in these lists, you can get an idea of average page length, price, and the pros and cons of each book via Amazon reviews.

Other resources on Amazon include Amazon Charts,[5] which provides the top 20 most read and most sold books in the fiction and non-fiction categories, respectively. Amazon also provides lists of bestsellers from the current year going back to 1995. You can synthesize all this data by checking out their most popular product of the year page.[6]

Barnes & Noble

While Amazon is the largest online retailer for books, Barnes and Noble is the largest brick-and-mortar retailer. This Fortune 500 company has been in business for over a century and is still going strong, generating revenue despite the turbulent atmosphere of the book retail business. Even though Barnes and Noble have retail stores in all 50 states of the U.S., their website is a nice source of market research data for authors.[7]

BookGraph[8] provides an interesting way to search by clicking on a title and seeing a visual map of connected books. Discover Categories[9] provides a list of categories and their subcategories. B&N Top 100[10] provides a list of the top 100 books from favorite authors. You also have the capability of clicking on various subjects in the left column and getting the top 100 books for those specific subjects as well. For example, clicking on Science & Technology will provide you with the top Science & Technology Bestsellers.[11] Barnes & Noble Stores Bestsellers[12] provide several lists of the bestselling books across the country. You can filter the lists by fiction, non-fiction, paperback and more.

Even though Amazon and Barnes & Noble are the largest online and brick- and-mortar book businesses, you should definitely consider using other online retail outlets for helpful market research data. Places in which you can find different lists of books are Wal-Mart,[13] Target Books,[14] Powell's[15], and eBay,[16] to name a few.

New York Times Best Sellers and More

The New York Times Best Sellers[17] list is considered one of the most prestigious lists of its kind in the United States. Even though N.Y. Times Best Sellers is considered the eminent list in the U.S., it doesn't mean that it's error-proof. Like many lists, it has been subjugated to some manipulation tactics and has been criticized for not being 100% accurate.

Regardless of the various opinions about accuracy, The New York Times bestseller site is an excellent resource for market research. It contains several lists of various categories broken down by fiction, non-fiction, hardcover, paperback, and a combination of various formats, such as print and e-book. It makes it convenient for self-publishers to discover popular topics that can serve as a muse for their next book.

You can analyze multiple bestseller lists from various publishing sources, like Publishers Weekly,[18] USA Today,[19] Los Angeles Times,[20] Indiebound,[21] Thriftbooks,[22] Penguin Random House, [23] Audible,[24] Hudson Booksellers,[25] and Books-A-Million,[26] to name a few. These additional bestseller lists can help you cross-check against the N.Y. Times Best Sellers. You'll inevitably discover books that are common and uncommon across the lists.

Magazines

Every time you have waited in an office setting, there are magazines to help you pass the time. However, the next time you're waiting in an office, you'll look at magazines in a different light. You can use them to help brainstorm ideas for future books. The good news is that you don't have to rush to the nearest office to discover magazine ideas. You could simply go on the web and visit Magazines.com.[27] Not only does this site provide discounts on various magazines, but it also serves as an excellent source for market research as it provides a list of the best-selling magazines, along with categorized lists. There are also filtering options on the site so that you can refine the results by price, rating, and bestsellers.

Goodreads

This online social cataloging site has been acquired by Amazon. Not only does it help authors gain more traction with their books, which will be explained in more detail in Chapter Six, but it's also a great site to use for market research. I recommend spending time on their Listopia page, which is a dedicated page to various book reading lists.[28] You'll discover lists for "Best of"[29] which breaks down best books by all time, year, decade, and century. You can also discover the most popular book lists,[30] which features such interesting curated lists that, if you're not careful enough, will make you want to go into book reading mode.

Using Search Engines

The primary focus of search engines is to match information. Something that authors should pay attention to are the keywords that best describe the information in their book.

For example, Star Wars can be classified as science fiction/fantasy, while Harry Potter can be classified as fantasy, urban fantasy, and contemporary fantasy. Having a specific list of keywords is excellent for magnifying discoverability.

If you're struggling thinking of the keywords, then you can use the search engines *autocomplete* feature. This is a search completion feature activated when you start typing in search queries. To test it yourself, type in a general keyword best describing the content of a popular title in a search engine of your choice. While you're typing, this should trigger some keywords via autocomplete. The search engine should provide a list of keyword suggestions that could be used to help promote your book.

You can also use multiple search engines to cross reference each other. Some popular search engines are Google, Bing, and DuckDuckGo. Also, don't forget the search engines embedded in popular ecommerce sites, like Amazon or Barnes and Noble.

As you search for keywords, start off with broad topics as the auto feature will help provide more specific keywords that could best describe the content of your book. Starting off with too specific or *long tail keywords* will often provide you with zero keywords via auto complete.

BISAC

The Book Industry Study Group (BISG)[31] created a classification for physical and digital books known as the BISAC code. This is a nine-character alphanumeric code that corresponds to an industry-approved list of subject descriptions. This can be useful for brick-and-mortar stores to figure out where to place books on shelves, or it can be used to discover which genres to place the books under in an online database. There's a complete list of subject headings along with their corresponding codes on the complete BISAC subject headings[32] part of their site.

These codes are good to know when you decide which topic to write your book about since they are used by many top companies in the book industry. BISAC also provides a hypertextual list of book topics that could help inspire your writing.

Eyes & Ears

When all else fails, listen with your eyes and ears. Since I do a lot of traveling, I like to keep an eye out for businesses in the area. Cities like Los Angeles and New York City are fashion-centric, so if you take a walk down Garment District or the famous Rodeo Drive, then you'll have no issues pinpointing boutiques and various specialty clothing stores. Local authors who have an interest in fashion may consider the possibility of writing a fashion-related book to cater to the desires of these demographics. Places that you want to pay attention to are areas with significant foot traffic. Shopping malls are generally good places to start.

You can also cross-reference your discoveries by entering the right queries in search engines, like: "biggest industries in [city]." Replace the keyword *city* with the location you want to investigate. For example, "biggest industries in houston texas" is an example of such a search query.

After searching this term in Google, I was able to find a page on the City of Houston site that listed the major economy and trade sectors in the area.[33] These type of government websites are credible sources to refer to when learning about the economy of a geographic area.

I'm a big coffee drinker and thus find refuge in coffee shops. I can grab my favorite drink, a bite to eat and get work done or chat with a friend. Conversations are a big part of going to coffee shops, and I occasionally find myself engrossed in discussions about purchasing real estate, how to eat healthier, politics, traveling to exotic locations, and the list goes on. These conversations are topics that can be expanded upon in a book.

Conversations are not limited to coffee shops; they can also take place anywhere where people congregate, such as supermarkets, events, and restaurants. Naturally, all conversations are not book material, but just keep an ear out for potential topics for a book, especially if it's a recurring topic you find yourself involved in.

Just a reminder: you shouldn't let a conversation or two dictate whether you write a book about a certain topic, as writing a book is a time intensive process. Instead, it can serve as a starting point for further research which you can cross-check with sites like Amazon or Barnes & Noble.

Prototyping Your Dream

Like with any business, there's no guarantee your book will do well. There are multiple variables that determine the success of a book, including the title, cover, and content, as well as how strong the marketing campaign is. Even good books need a push to generate the interest of the masses.

With that being said, you should test the waters before you make the commitment of writing a book. Gauge the demand for your potential book and how competitive the market will be. The more competition generally means the more expensive the advertising will be for your genre, and this creates a higher barrier for entry into the industry. However, competitive markets typically mean higher earning potential that could be a worthwhile tradeoff.

Test how marketable your book idea is by creating a prototype. Luckily there are low-cost, low-tech, and affordable ways to go about doing this.

Here are all of the ingredients you'll need: web building software, email marketing software, web analytics, and paid advertising (like Google AdWords). The purpose of this is to quickly put together a landing page describing the theme of your book and use it to collect email addresses. Doing so will measure how interested prospective readers are about your book topic.

Decide which web-publishing platform to use: If you want to get something quickly up and running, then using a free web-hosting platform might be perfect for you. There are many available solutions. The most popular are Wix,[34] Blogger,[35] and Wordpress.[36]

One thing you should think twice about before deciding is whether your website can obtain analytics. A popular free web analytic software is Google Analytics[37] and it's not possible to use with Wix without upgrading to premium since a custom URL is needed.[38] However, there are alternative analytics apps available in the Wix marketplace that you can consider.[39] With Blogger you can easily integrate Google Analytics with your blog,[40] and if you're using a free Wordpress.com blog, then there's a stats feature[41] available to you.

Create a landing page: Think about what you would want your prospective customer to see. You will want the visitor to take some type of action on your site so that you can calculate how well their actions convert. A simple thing to do is have an email form so you can collect their email. In order to entice them to do this, you might want to consider providing them a digital gift of some type, like a sample chapter of your book once it's available. You can use an email service like MailChimp[42] to collect emails of visitors to your site. For tips from Google on how to build a better landing page, read: *Understanding landing page experience.*[43]

Post an ad on AdWords: The last step in the equation is to post ads on Google AdWords to get traffic to your site. You can advertise any URL, even a Facebook page, as long as it adheres to the Google AdWords advertising policy.[44] After all, it's difficult to test, track, and interpret data without any visitors to your site. With AdWords you will have to pay per click, and this may not seem worthwhile in the beginning, but if you can get some concrete data to pre-test the validity of your book idea, wouldn't that data be golden? You can ask friends and family for their input, or even make online posts soliciting opinions from experts, but none of this is more telling than having verifiable data from an actual marketing campaign. After your campaign is done, you'll have better insights into how much it will cost to advertise your site in the genre and how in-demand the content for your prospective book is.

CHAPTER II:
The Practical Writing Process

Do me a favor and take a trip down memory lane. Remember how much you dreaded writing essays in school? Now, look at you thinking about writing your very own book! Are you confused on how to get started in the writing process? Do you suffer consistently from writer's block? Are you afraid to write anything because the thought of you sounding silly makes you cringe? Take a deep breath and find solace that you're far from the only writer to experience these thoughts.

The good news is that there are certain steps you can follow to help increase the productivity of your writing. I think I'm qualified to speak on this as I've self-published three books and counting and have written a plethora of e-books in the past.

Just like any skill, the more you invest in it, the more you get out. At one point in your life, you couldn't stabilize your motion on a bicycle. When you were an infant, your legs weren't strong enough to support your weight. Both obstacles are now non-existent. The same thing can be said about your writing woes. I'm going to reveal to you the system that has helped me dramatically increase my writing productivity. I'll also reveal beneficial resources that will help make you a more skillful writer.

Pre-drafting

Every writer, including some of the best writers of all time, runs into obstacles with writing. I agree with the notion that ideas don't always flow easily, and writer's block is something that truly does exist. However, if a writer waits for inspiration to come before they write, then at best they'll be constantly submitting late work.

Instead, writers must devise a mechanism to help combat mental paralysis and get ideas to flow naturally like water. These are time-tested principles that work. To get the best results, I would recommend that you give them an honest go.

When I first started writing, I thought the idea of investing significant time into the pre-drafting phase was counterintuitive. I would think, "Why invest so much time in the pre-drafting phase when the goal of writing is to produce quality text?" I would instead dive head first and start building a table of contents as the outline and then desperately try fill it in. What happened was that the table of contents evolved so much over the course of writing the book that the finished TOC was virtually unrecognizable from its predecessor. Foregoing the pre-drafting phase caused me significant harm in the long haul as it stymied the writing process and caused me to write in a disorganized manner. Therefore, every time I now write a book, I always invest significant time in the pre-drafting phase. Here are some proven principles to test to help facilitate this process.

Free writing: This is a technique that helps you get rid of any symptoms of writer's block by literally writing whatever comes to mind. Elements of writing that you may take into account in your final work such as spelling, punctuation, grammar, and flow should all be ignored. The purpose of this technique is to write as much content as quickly and fast as possible. In other words, you just want to cast a wide net; you're not necessarily concerned about making too much sense about what you write as even nonsensical things could help provide that creative spark you need for another topic later.

So that's the goal. Simply take out a piece of paper, pen, and timer and then write continuously for the allocated amount of time about a topic. If you can't think of anything to write, then literally write, "I can't think of anything." Again, one of the benefits to this task is to get comfortable with writing uninhibited because no one will see your free writing unless you want them to. If you're a new writer, I would recommend practicing daily free writing sessions so you can become more comfortable dumping out what's in your mind. Start out with five minute sessions and then steadily work your way up to 30 minute sessions. The purpose of this is to create a mental-sprint to try and let the thoughts in your head transfer freely to paper.

Brainstorming: This is similar to free writing in that the goal is to provide an uncut and unedited transcription of what's in your mind to paper.

However, what's different is the structuring of the writing. The goal when you brainstorm is to provide short sentences, typically in a bulleted format. This is different compared to free writing as words are grouped into sentences. The process in which you can practice your brainstorming skills is the same exact process you would follow with free writing, but instead, jot down a list of ideas that come to mind. Don't worry about correctness or how connected the ideas are as this is something that you can fix later.

Mind maps: This technique might be more suitable for visual learners as this technique uses images to organize information. Mind maps are typically created around a single topic which is drawn as an image in the center of the page. Then related topics are drawn and connected to the center of the image. These sub-topics may also have sub-topics of their own and thus spawn their own branches.

Mind mapping can be used alone or after you've conducted some free writing sessions; you can take topics that you wish to further investigate and draw mind maps for them. Mind maps have a wide array of applications. They can be used to help someone make decisions, absorb new learning material, or even decide what to do in a new city. There are many mind mapping tools that a writer can make use of, such as XMind,[1] FreeMind,[2] and Freeplane.[3]

Drafting

This is the phase in which the writer attempts to compose the first version of their book. In other words, the author attempts to give their book some form and shape. To help picture this, think of the evolutionary process in which a home is constructed. There are many stages to it, but the homeowner can begin to see a shape once the framework is established.

In this phase of the book writing process, it's time to add text to your document. Before you enter this point, you should have some notes to kick-start the drafting process. This is one reason why it's very important to invest time in the pre-drafting or planning phase. It will make opening up a blank canvas look less intimidating. However, starting the writing process is a peculiar thing. Even if writers have notes, they may still struggle getting into a writing rhythm. Rest assured that this is normal. I'll provide you with solid techniques to help get you started with adding form and character to your rough draft.

Paragraphing: Before we get into the details on what's involved with creating paragraphs, let's first understand the concept of what a paragraph is. According to the writing center of the University of Wisconsin-Madison, "paragraphs are effective building blocks to construct a complex analysis or argument."[4] A paragraph typically has a topic sentence which provides clues to what the paragraph is about, body sentences to develop the topic, and a concluding sentence to bring the section to an end. The paragraph may also include transition sentences to help smoothly glide the reader from the preceding topic to the new one, or it may have linking sentences to help connect the ideas in the current paragraph to ideas in other paragraphs.

A book can be considered a summation of paragraphs that equates to one or more purposes. For example, the summation of the chapters of a book about "how to play an acoustic guitar" should educate a reader about principles on how to play the instrument. The chapters of a book about the deforestation of the Amazon rainforest should, in totality, educate the reader about the impact of deforestation.

Do you remember the steps for writing a traditional five-paragraph essay in grade school? Each essay had an introduction, three body paragraphs, and a conclusion. It's a simple template that helps writers organize their thoughts and create logical arguments. You may also remember some of the rules your teacher may have reinforced, such as including three to five sentences per paragraph. This is not bad advice for someone venturing into writing, and it's even reinforced by Purdue OWL website.[5] However, what happens if you write a paragraph that's two sentences long or one that's twenty sentences? Is this a major error and should you consider revising it? Before we investigate further, I believe that the University of Bristol said it best: "There's no set rule for the appropriate amount of sentences in a paragraph."[6]

I believe that the reason why students start off with a predefined number for sentences in a paragraph is so that their ideas can be balanced. If certain paragraphs are longer than others, then that may be an indication that some ideas should be given more details than others. While I'm a firm believer of this, especially when writing full-sized books, writing a book is much longer and complicated than a five-paragraph essay. Keeping paragraphs balanced is more easily said than done. Some ideas will naturally be more important than others and therefore the paragraph size will reflect that. In the process of writing a book, it's unreasonable to assume that all paragraphs will be balanced because there are too many ideas which all have varying degrees of importance.

Keep in mind that you're allowed to write your paragraphs in any order you want. I typically don't write my books in a linear manner, but instead prefer to build the chapters in an intermittent order. I tend to have a good vision of how the shape of the book will look through an intensive pre-drafting phase. It's almost like assembling multiple chunks of a puzzle in isolation, and then integrating them together at the end to complete the conundrum.

Time-boxing: A technique that helps get me in the groove of writing is time-boxing. Over the course of a writing project, I will test varying write-and-rest combinations, but the one I prefer most is writing for 30 minutes and then resting for five minutes. This work/rest ratio helps me produce content in a sustainable manner. I write non-stop for a set period of time and then take consistent breaks to prevent overworking myself, minimizing burnout.

Shaking things up: In a modern society, the average person spends a significant amount of time in front of a computer. I prefer to spend some time writing on old-fashioned paper. I have no scientific evidence to back this up, but it helps me facilitate the writing process. The speed in which I'm able to get through the pre-drafting phase is faster using pen and paper compared to that of a word processor. I also know that I will spend a lot of time writing on the computer, so it allows me to shake things up and prevent boredom.

I also like switching from computer to traditional paper/pen if the affliction of writer's block settles in. By switching mediums, ideas seem to flow more smoothly. In addition to switching up what I'm writing on, I also like to adjust where I'm writing. One day my preference for a writing environment may be a quiet setting like a home office, and on another day, it could be in a more social setting like a co-working space in the heart of the city.

Filibustering: Have you experimented with the free writing technique, but still suffer from vexatious writer's block? If so, then you can use the audio version of free writing and instead of continuously writing, you can record yourself talking about the topic. A couple of tools to assist you with this process are iTunes Voice Recorder & Audio Editor (iOS),[7] and Smart Recorder (Android).[8] This is akin to performing a filibuster with the exception that there's thankfully no political affiliation. Another variation of this technique is to type on your computer nonstop for a set amount of time. You may find that one method gives better results over another, so it's important that you test different variations to see which one works best for you.

Revision

Once you have completed your draft, it's time to officially enter the revision phase. The revision process can be described as an iterative process in which changes to your draft are made. Through this evolutionary process, a new draft emerges at a higher quality than its predecessor.

It's typically not done in one setting. Instead, multiple revisions are needed to get things "right." It's important to note that revisions are not the same as editing, in which mechanical elements of the document are corrected. Instead, revision focuses more on the big picture, how a document can be improved. Here are some tips on what to consider in making revisions for your document.

Does it fulfill your goal? When an author produces a book, there should be an objective they're trying to accomplish. Authors shouldn't write for the sake of reaching a word count because doing so would result in meaningless text that has no use for the reader. The summation of all the paragraphs in a book should help the author reach their intended goal. If not, then careful revision is mandatory.

Are topics well-organized? Do the ideas of a book progress in a logical and coherent manner? Some writers may write books in reverse chronological order as a literary technique. For example, instead of the scenes progressing A through Z, they flow from Z through A to increase dramatic effect. However, using this format for a book teaching the reader to play an acoustic guitar doesn't make sense. In this case the topics should be ordered in a way that logically build on top of one another so the reader can make micro-achievements and stay motivated to continue learning.

Extra toppings or light cheese? Are certain paragraphs too short and need more detail to make the point stronger? Or are these paragraphs better served being integrated into other paragraphs? Conversely, are some paragraphs unnecessarily bulky and need trimming or need to be broken into additional paragraphs? These are questions to consider in the revision stage.

Is it well-formed? If you have a printed copy of your draft and are trying to revise it by reading through it, do you find any awkward wording, excessively repeated words, confusing descriptions, wordy explanations, or uninspiring-sleep-inducing blocks of text? If so, then consider rewriting it asap. Are the font size and types appropriate and consistent throughout the text? Pay attention to these matters and make proper adjustments so that the document is consistent.

Editing

This is the final stage of the writing process before the author can proceed to the publication stage. Remember, there's a difference between revising and editing your document. Revision is much more immersive as questions are asked and clarity is demanded. While certain things like word choice are looked at, the more mechanical portion is reserved for the editing phase. The focus in this stage is spelling, punctuation, grammar, and word choice. A proper editing process ensures that a book is written in correct conventions in accordance to the language that it's published in.

In the past, I would mix revision with the editing process, but after writing a couple of books, I'm a believer in reserving the bulk of editing until the end. The reason for this is that if you edit your content before you finish revising the draft, you may end up cutting content that you invested significant time editing. This throws many man hours out the window, which is not something I personally recommend. Therefore, to avoid the possibility of editing content that you won't use, I would recommend reserving the majority of it until the final stage. Below are some tips on how to properly edit your book.

Read it loud & slowly: If you plan on editing your book by reading it in a quiet setting, I would recommend against it. The reason being is that you already have an idea of what you're trying to say and are vulnerable to overlooking misspellings or grammar errors. Therefore, to decrease the chances of this happening, read your book loudly and slowly and be actively engaged in it. Don't just nonchalantly read it; pay attention to every word and to the context.

Editing your own document can be tricky at times. Spell checkers are great tools, but I would recommend relying on human edited documents first and then using spell checkers as an extra layer of protection. The reason for this is that spell checkers can give false positives/negatives, or sometimes miss out on errors altogether. A tool you can use to reinforce correct grammar of the book after you get a pair of human eyes on it is Grammarly.[9]

Multiple sets of eyes: As mentioned previously, editing your own document can be a chore. Instead, try and get multiple eyes on the document because some errors can be difficult to detect, even to the most discerning eye. Therefore, you could consider reaching into your networks and soliciting for reviewers to look over your document. They could perhaps help detect errors that you may have not noticed in the first go-around.

If this is not a feasible option, then you could consider outsourcing this task. A good network to find talent is UpWork.com.[10] There are many types of editors out there, so it's important to know the difference if you are looking for the right person to do the job.

A *copy editor* is like your buddy in the publication process. They don't just cover the mechanical details, they also help you revise your document by improving readability and accuracy of your text. It's okay to go back between the various parts of the writing process. For example, if something is detected as being inaccurate in later phases, then you could go back to the pre-drafting phase to double-check accuracy.

A *proofreader* is the person who sees the last version of the document before its *okayed* for the publication process. In layman terms, a proofreader acts as quality insurance at the end of the production line. They inspect the final product, which will be a galley proof to confirm that no errors have sneaked its way into the final publication. Example of tasks that a proofreader will look for are poor graphics quality and incorrect numbering of pages.

While a proofreader may do line editing, like correcting a comma splice or inconsistent naming conventions, this is the job of the copy editor. If too many typographical/grammatical errors are discovered, then the document may be passed back to the copy editor for another look through.

The proofreader is especially critical for mass published books. Let's say that a company prints 10,000 copies of a book with glaring errors. Can you imagine that this a costly error? Proofreaders are supposed to prevent these types of issues from manifesting into the manuscript. They can be seen as a liaison between the author and the publication company. Some authors may even decide to hire multiple proofreaders as an extra layer of protection. Since most self-publishers that use print-on-demand process are on a tight budget, utilizing a proofreader may not be an economical option. Instead, most self-publishers opt for copying editing services solely.

Modified Kanban for Writing

In my junior year of college, I took a course on software engineering. We were assembled into peer groups and needed to collaborate in order to finish challenging tasks. In retrospective, this class helped prepare students for the workforce as many software engineering jobs programmers are put into groups and must work together as a single cohesive unit to reach project deadlines. However, simply putting a bunch of programmers into groups and telling them to get the job done by a certain date is apathetic management. A process must be executed to give the developers the best chance possible of reaching the targeted goals. Goal planning, time-boxing and retrospection are utilized in many software project management frameworks to increase productivity and maximize timely project completion.

I'm a big fan of increasing productivity and even became certified in *Scrum*, a popular project management framework for software development. It was derived largely from *Kanban*, which is a system used by Toyota to increase productivity in their manufacturing process.

Over the course of time, I've extracted elements from Kanban and blended it into the way I produce books. One of the first things I do when I decide to write a book is to figure out what topics make it into the book. In the past, I would try to create a comprehensive table of contents and outline upfront.

However, over the course of time, I decided to deviate from this strategy as I found out that the content that makes it to the final draft of a book is too volatile. In other words, the content of my books changed so significantly over the course of time that I decided creating a table of contents up front wasn't the way to go. Instead, I would apply a modified version of Kanban to the way I write. Here are the steps I take when figuring out what to write about in my books.

— **Gather appropriate materials.** I prefer to use multicolored sticky notes, pen/marker, a pack of index cards, a container for the cards, and a large surface to add the sticky notes to. If you don't have a large Whiteboard, then that's okay; you can use any large surface in which you can add sticky notes to. An example of one is a large, smooth wall in your room so that your sticky notes won't slide off. The point of this is to create what's known as a Kanban board which will be explained in detail shortly. However, I would highly recommend finding a large surface as doing so will help provide you an eagle-eye view of the details of your project, which for me is crucial when it comes to figuring out what needs to be added, removed, or re-organized.

— **Build inventory of topics.** As mentioned previously, the beginning of a new writing project is tentative. From my experience, the table of contents would change so dramatically from beginning to end that trying to structure and order it proved counterproductive. Instead, I just dump all of the topics that will go into the book on sticky notes. What I'll do is scan through my free writing, brainstorming, and mind-mapping sessions. I like to use all of them in order to force the words out of my head, but you're more than welcome to just use one if that's what you're comfortable with.

— Once I have the topics, I add them in large lettering to the sticky notes. It's important that you use large lettering on sticky notes as the point of this session is to be as frugal with your words as possible. This is supposed to be a fun and easy exercise to do some probing on potential topics that will make it in your book... nothing more, nothing less. The writing process is flexible in the beginning before you start writing anything, as changes to the project are generally easier and more convenient to make. So, feel free to go through this process without thinking too hard.

— Also, if you do decide to get multicolored sticky notes, then I would recommend making use of the color. The beauty is you can design whatever coding mechanism you want to use for the sticky notes. For example, you can designate blue to indicate that you need to research a topic, orange for writing about a topic, and yellow to imply that you're going to edit a topic. It's entirely up to you to determine how you will decide the coding mechanism.

— **Get the big picture:** Once you have a list of topics, the next step is to stick the topics on a large surface. This helps you better re-order the topics. The end goal of this practice is to cluster the related topics together. Once the topics are grouped, appropriately re-order them as logically as possible so that the flow of the book makes sense.

— When it comes to writing, the word, *"flow,"* refers to the cohesion of the content. Does the progression of the contents of the book seem logical? For example, if you're writing a book about the fundamentals of playing basketball, it's probably not a good idea to start off teaching the jump shot when there's many less advanced subjects the author should discuss before that.

— **One bite at a time:** Before you can start estimating how long it will take for you to complete a task, you'll need to add more details to increase your chances of accuracy. Here's a technique you can consider. Grab a sticky note from your Kanban board, and then create an associated index card for it. On the front, write the name of the task, and then on the back, fill in the details that should be included within the topic. Going back to our previous example of basketball, if you want to add more details about a section in the book involving "how to increase basketball dribbling skills," you may include topics such as:

— Dribbling techniques for beginners
— How to dribble faster
— Types of dribbling
— How to dribble between your legs
— Basketball dribbling tricks
— Dribbling drills
— Basics of dribbling

- Moving with the basketball
- Tips on dribbling

After you've added in the topics you can re-order, structure, and extend the topics. Here's an example of the content re-ordered and structured:
- Dribbling
  - Basics of dribbling
  - How to dribble
  - Moving and dribbling
  - Stopping and driving
    - Types of dribbles
    - Crossover dribble
    - Behind the back dribbling
    - Between the legs crossover
    - Reverse crossover
- Basketball dribbling tricks
- Dribbling exercises

As you can see some topics were added and some were consolidated into larger topics to make the flow more logical. It's important to get granular and break down the topics into as many reasonable subtopics as possible. Doing so will make writing longer chapters seem less daunting as you're breaking it into smaller, more modular units. The motto I love using to describe this is: "eat the elephant one bite at a time."

Estimating your work: Once you have divided the topics into as many subtopics as possible, now comes the time for estimating your tasks. If this is your first book, then you will most likely be a little inaccurate with your estimates as you don't have previous work to reference. You have no baseline, which is why I recommend breaking your topics down into as many subtopics possible. Once you've estimated each task individually, sum them all up to get a gauge of how long it will take for you to write the book.

Retrospection: This is probably one of the most important things that you can do in terms of improving your writing. Every week I would highly recommend investing time into analyzing your writing process. Ask yourself what went well, what can be improved upon, and what changes you're going to make next week. All the changes you'll make in the upcoming weeks could be added to your inventory of things to do.

The purpose of the Kanban board is to allow you to see the progress you're making daily. You do this by creating three columns that shows the state of work, which are: "To Do," "Doing," and "Done." When you first start a new project, the sticky notes will be loaded in the "To Do" column, and then once you know what tasks you'll be working on, the sticky notes will transition from the "To Do" column to the "Doing" one. Once the task is complete, it will transfer to the "Done" column. This allows you to see the progression of the work you're making. In an ideal world, once you're done, all of the sticky notes will transfer to the "Done" column. However, products are very rarely done in the true sense of the word. Constant upgrades are being made, and defects are found and patched. It's a continuous and evolutionary process that products undergo, so in actuality, work is constantly being added. If you want to use software that can assist you with task-planning, then popular choices are Evernote[11] or Trello.[12]

Front & back matter: To make your book look more professional, I recommend adding a title page, copyright page, and index. The title page goes before the copyright page and contains the title, subtitle, author, imprint, publisher, and date of publication. The copyright page typically follows the title page and contains the copyright notice, publication information, legal notices, cataloging information, and ISBN (explained in next chapter). Toward the end of the book is where the index should be placed. A published book should definitely have a carefully curated index. Including one helps readers to more easily locate specific content in the book. If you're creating your book using Microsoft Word, then you can easily create your table of contents as it has a feature just for this process. You can read the "How to create a table of contents by marking text in word"[13] article for tips on how to create a table of contents in Word.

Cheat Sheet for the Writing Process

Create a loose plan for the writing you are to do. The plan should be specific enough so you can get started, but flexible enough so that any unforeseeable change won't cause major disorder in the writing process. Ironically, the first step in the writing phase, known as *pre-drafting*, doesn't require you to even open your word processor. In this phase, you generate as many topics for your book as possible. I prefer free writing with paper and pen, but you can choose any writing platform you want.

- When you start crafting content for your book, this is known as the *drafting* phase. The book begins to form a more lucid picture as the author edges closer to producing their manuscript. Don't worry about writing too much as there will be plenty of opportunities to fix this in subsequent stages.
- Revise your document. Improve order, flow, style, wording, and clarity. Writing is a cyclic process and its normal to iterate forward and backward in the writing phases
    - Repeat the previous step as much as necessary. A more lucid picture of your book should emerge overtime.
    - Reorder, re-shape, and rewrite as much as possible. Skimpy paragraphs have more details added or are integrated into other paragraphs; bulky paragraphs are trimmed and made more readable. Paragraphs are checked to ensure they contribute to the overall quality of the book.
- Revision and editing are occasionally used interchangeably, but they are traditionally distinct roles in the publishing industry. Reserving the bulk of editing until the end is ideal as writers can prevent investing time in fixing up content that will ultimately get deleted.
- Repeat this phase until errors are eradicated and a higher-class book manifests.

CHAPTER III:
The Birth of a Book

To produce a book mimicking the quality of N.Y. Times bestsellers, there are two things you need to get right: the interior design and the book cover. The interior design is concerned with the internal details of the book, while the book cover deals with the outside portion of a book. There are many more specifications that you need to know to put the ideas you have about your book into publication. This chapter will equip you with all the info you'll need to confidently go through the publication process.

Trim Sizes

The *trim size* refers to the physical dimensions of a book. For an e-book, this is not concerning as they're typically dynamic, or variable, in dimensions. The same e-book could render on a smart phone, tablet, or laptop, which will most likely all have different screen sizes. However, physical things have shape to them, and for this you'll need to know their dimensions. All trim sizes are listed in a *width x height* format. Different print-on-demand companies offer varying options for trim sizes. For example, CreateSpace offers seven standard sizes[1] for paperbacks while IngramSpark offers fourteen trim sizes for hard covers. Which one to use boils down to the genre of your book.

For example, if you plan on creating a textbook, then you will want a larger trim size, something like 8 x 10". If you plan on writing a general fiction book, then 5.25 x 8" is a safe choice. If you plan on creating an inspirational book, then 5 x 8" is a popular choice. My advice is to pay attention to the trim sizes of books in your niche. It's probably not a good idea to be much smaller or larger than the average trim size, but somewhere in the middle is a better option.

If you're absolutely confused about which trim size to choose, then my advice is to default to 6 x 9". This is a nice trim size, especially if you're planning to sell to bookstores in which your cover needs to be displayed. When you choose 6 x 9", it's big enough to clearly depict your book cover, which is one of your biggest marketing paths in bookstores. It's also small enough so that the book will fit on the shelves with no problems.

Think about the economy of the trim size. For example, smaller books tend to lose more space to margins while 6 x 9" books can fill in more text on each page with their larger page sizes. This could save a self-publisher excess expense when producing the book. If all pages cost the same to print and a self-publisher uses a smaller trim size when a 6 x 9" one would suffice, then the book will be more expensive to produce due to more pages. Once you have decided what trim size to use, you can further think about the interior of your book.

ISBNs: The Social Security Number for Books

The Social Security Number (SSN) was created back in 1936 with the original purpose of tracking financial information of U.S. Workers. However, it has expanded significantly since its inception and is now used virtually as a universal identifier and is assigned to an individual at birth. It allows various government agencies to identify individuals in their records.[2] Books have their variant of a SSN and it's called an International Standard Book Number (ISBN). An ISBN can be defined as a country assigned unique 13-digit number[3] that uniquely identifies a specific edition of a book. Just like how a SSN can track a U.S. citizen's work or financial history, an ISBN can be used to track the history of a book. Wholesalers, distributors, and bookstores can use the ISBN to track the book's history.

Like how an SSN identifies an individual so they won't be mixed up with someone else, an ISBN provides specific details about a particular book so that it won't be confused with another.

Title, edition, format, and page numbers are some of the details that are encoded with an ISBN.

ISBNs assigned on or after January 1, 2007 are 13-digits and those assigned before that date were 10-digits. Depending on the country of the author, the price of the ISBN will vary. For example, countries like Canada and India freely distribute ISBNs to their authors, while countries like the U.S. and Australia charge for their ISBN.

In addition to having varying prices by countries, ISBNs also have different agencies responsible for distributing them. In Canada ISBNs are distributed by a government agency, while in the United States it's a privately held company responsible for this—that company is R.R Bowker, colloquially known as Bowker. U.S.-based authors can purchase ISBNs at various price points in quantities as listed below:[4]

- 1 ISBN: $125
- 10 ISBNs: $295
- 100 ISBNs: $575
- 1000 ISBNs: $1500

If you're working on a shoestring budget, then you may be wondering if you need your own ISBN number. The answer is contingent on your marketing strategy. For example, if you only intend to distribute your book through Amazon KDP and CreateSpace, then you don't need your own ISBN. The reason being is that Amazon provides self-publishers the option to use an Amazon Standard Identification Number (ASIN),[5] and CreateSpace provides authors with the option of using a CreateSpace-Assigned ISBN.[6] However, if authors have a plan to make their printed books available to book stores or retailers, then they must have their own ISBN.

If authors want to use other e-book distribution services outside Amazon KDP, like iBooks, then they'll need their own unique ISBN. In layman terms, owning your own ISBN costs you money but opens up doors to more marketing opportunities. Also, if you plan on publishing multiple books in various formats, then consider starting off with the 10 ISBN package to save money as you save when purchasing in bulk as opposed to purchasing each ISBN individually. For example, if you publish an e-book, hardcover, paperback, and audiobook version to a title, then you'll need a unique ISBN for each separate format, or four ISBNs in total.

You can assign titles to your ISBNs through your MyIdentifiers account.[7] The website, isbn.org, is owned by Bowkers and will redirect you to a separate site they own, MyIdentifiers, in which you can purchase ISBNs. You can also purchase barcodes here, which will be discussed in further detail in the next section. I would recommend creating a business/marketing plan for your book before you make your final decision to purchase your own ISBN or to use one assigned by a distributor. Once an ISBN is matched to a title, it can't be changed unless significant modifications are made to the book. For example, a new edition of a previous title would warrant a new ISBN, but changing the price wouldn't.

Barcodes

This is an optical machine readable representation of data that describes something about the item that carries the code. It's important to note that a barcode is not the same as an ISBN. An ISBN is an identifier for your book while a barcode is a graphical representation of your ISBN and price of your book. Bowker, or the agency that's responsible for issuing ISBNs to U.S.-based publishers, also sell barcodes. According to their website, "Bowker is the only US ISBN agency that ensures barcodes meets all the latest requirements of the publishing industry."[8] You can purchase barcodes from the same site you get ISBNs which is MyIdentifiers. They're priced $25 per barcode if you purchase 1-5, $23 per barcode if purchasing 6-10, or $21 per barcode if 11+ are purchased. [9]

Barcodes are only used for physical products; it allows checkout scanners to associate a price with a book. It's an efficient way for merchants to keep track of inventory. ISBNs can be used for both electronic and physical books, while barcodes are only used for printed books. Therefore, if you only plan to sell your book through Amazon KDP, then a barcode is not needed, but if you plan on distributing your book through retail outlets like Barnes & Noble, then a barcode is required. Barcodes typically go on the lower right hand corner of your book and are 2.00 x 1.25". It's important that this area of the back cover is clear of any text or images to prevent distorting the barcode.

Interior

A professionally designed interior helps give your book the mark of credibility. Appropriate font style, sizes, and layout all help make your book more readable. You want readers to complete your book as the more it's read, the higher the chances of getting your book reviewed. Even though I would highly recommend outsourcing the task of getting the interior of your book designed, there are still some decisions you'll have to make as the self-publisher. Some of these are what paper type to use, whether the book should be printed in color or black and white, or if your margins will bleed.

Black & white or color? To be truly honest, getting your book printed in full color is very expensive when using a print-on-demand service. I recommend that self-publishers avoid this unless they are creating a book in which color is the industry norm. For example, children's books are typically done in color. To help offset the expensive costs of full-colored books, children's books are typically short, usually less than 40 pages, so creating a full-colored children's book is within reach of self-publishers. For example, with CreateSpace books, 110-828 pages costs $0.012 per page. However, for full-colored books, 42-500 pages costs $0.07 per page,[10] which is five times the cost of black and white. Therefore, only when its industry normative should full-colored books be the primary option for self-publishers.

Paper types: There are two primary paper types: white and cream. Even though there's no standardization on when to use white versus cream paper, a general rule of thumb is that when a book is purely textual, like a novel, then use cream paper. If the book contains images like screenshots or diagrams, then use white paper. The reason for this is that books with images purportedly print better on white paper. There may be some validity to this theory as the only paper option for colored books is white paper—the whiteness helps create a stronger contrast.

Also, keep in mind that different print-on-demand services will output a different quality of print. For example, the print quality for cream paper in CreateSpace is not identical to the one for Lightning Source. The only way to guarantee which print output you'll like best is to do a test run at the POD services you're considering. Cream paper tends to be heavier than white paper. If an author is trying to calculate the spine for their book, there are two different formulas used for cream and white paper. Books that use cream paper will have a slightly thicker spine than their white paper counterparts.

Bleeding pages: Don't worry. This is not as scary as it sounds. In printing, bleeding refers to when images or elements of a page touch the edge, extending past the trim edge and thus leaving no margin. To understand this better, we need to understand the limitations of printers. Since printers have a difficult time printing to the edge of paper, bleeding is a technique that can assist with this. The paper that's used for printing will be slightly larger than the selected trim size. In this way, after print is done the page can be trimmed down to the actual trim size, and the images have the appearance of extending past one or more of the edges. Bleeding can be applied to anything that must be printed such as business or postcards. If you do decide to use bleeds, then the dimensions for your book will be slightly larger. Here's the formula for calculating the new dimensions of a book with bleed added:

Height = bleed + height of book + bleed

Width = width of book + bleed

The bleed of a book is equal to ⅛ inch or 0.125. Therefore, the dimension of a 6 x 9" inch book, according to the above formula with bleed, is 6.125 x 9.25".

File types for book interiors: Once you have figured out the trim size and paper type for your book, the next step is to figure out if you will be selling an e-book and printed version of your book. If you plan on selling an e-book on Amazon KDP, then there is a myriad of formats that they accept. The supported files, along with their descriptions, can be found on the "Supported e-book Formats" page:[11]
- Word (DOC/ DOCX)
- HTML (ZIP, HTM, HTML)
- MOBI
- ePub
- RTF
- TXT
- PDF

As a general rule of thumb, I recommend creating an EPUB file if having an electronic book is critical to your marketing plan. This file format opens the doors to your electronic distribution possibilities significantly. EPUB is the abbreviation for *electronic publication* and its file extension is .epub. It's a technical standard for the International Digital Publishing Forum (IDPF) and became an official standard of IDPF since 2007. It's widely supported by an array of devices, such as: computers, tablets, e-readers, and smart phones. IDPF endorses EPUB 3 as the format of choice when it comes to packaging content.[12] Compared to pdf, EPUB3 is better optimized for the screens of computing devices. A popular open source tool that's commonly used when creating EPUBs is Calibre.[13]

If you plan on having a physical version of your book, then you need a corresponding pdf file. Designers typically prefer Adobe InDesign[14] to create high quality pdfs for print as opposed to Microsoft Word, which provides design limitations. I recommend delegating the work of the interior file to that of a skilled designer. You want to look for someone who has experience designing EPUB files for KDP and using Adobe InDesign for creating pdf files for print. There are many designers available that can do this for you on a contractual basis.[15]

The details a designer will need to know to create the print file is the Word or .doc file, trim size, and if the pages will have bleed or not. It's also nice to reference any books of interior design you fancy.

If you're up for an adventure, then you can try and piece together the book interior yourself. You can download some book templates which CreateSpace provides in their community documents.[16]

Book Covers

Once the interior for your book is complete, you can finalize the book cover. If you're setting up your book for print, then you'll need to know how many pages will be in your book so you can compute the width of the spine. This is not something typically known until the interior of your book is done. I would recommend investing some heavy thinking into your cover as it's one of the strongest selling points for your book. I personally like to collaborate with skilled designers throughout this process. This way the designer will have a better picture of what I'm looking for and they can also provide suggestions on how to improve the designs. You can find professional book designers on Upwork.[17] You can also consider creating the book cover yourself. CreateSpace provides a tool to help you get started.[18]

Books for print need a front cover, spine, and back cover. At a minimum, the front cover should have the title of the book and the name of the author. The back cover should have a description of the book along with a barcode on the bottom right hand corner. The spine should have the title and author name. If there's space, then consider dropping the publishing company's logo on it. If you really want to get creative, consider a fun color scheme for the spine and any additive decorations that could make the spine stand out on a bookshelf. The key is to have a balance of graphics and text. Bear in mind that CreateSpace will only print text on spines with more than 130 pages. According to CreateSpace, there must be 0.0625" between the text and the edge of the spine.[19]

To complete your book for print, the spine's width must be computed. If you're using CreateSpace as a print-on-demand service, then the width is contingent on the page type and color. For example, if it's white paper, use *page count x .002252*, and if it's cream paper, use *page count x .0025*. Therefore, if a fiction black and white novel has 200 pages, and the author plans to print it using cream paper, then the width of its spine should be *200 x .0025* or 0.5". For printed books, the cover image should be one file. Therefore, the front cover, spine, and back cover should be a whole image as opposed to separate ones. The file extensions for book covers are JPEG or TIFF, and should be at least 300 dots per inch (dpi). Resolutions with less than 300 dpi will cause flags during the book submission process. That's not cool as I've learned from experience ;).

Now, there's another "type" of cover image that you should have. This is used for displaying the book cover for sale on Amazon. In this case, you'll only need the front cover of the book with the ideal specifications of 2,560 x 1,600 pixels and less than 50 MB.[20] Most e-book distribution services adapt Amazon's file requirements, so you can assume if your cover image is accepted in Amazon, then other e-book distribution services like Kobo, iBook, and Smashwords will do so as well.

Once you have the interior designed, you'll have what's known as the *manuscript*. This combined with the book cover will allow you to proceed to the printing process. It's typically a good idea to get what's known as a galley proof printed first, before okaying the sale of your printed book. The galley proof allows the proofreader one last chance to go through the physical book and ensure that there are no more errors left before it's released for sale. Once a book is printed, the changes are irreversible.

Cheat sheet for creating your book

The publication process can be completed once a saleable manuscript and cover are finished. Here are some tidbits to keep in mind:

- Figure out which formats of the books you will sell: e-book, printed, or both. My recommendation is to do both to increase your number of distribution options.
- Register ISBNs for your books. The website to do this for U.S.-based writers is Bowkers. It costs $125 for one and $250 for ten. Printed books and e-books get separate ISBNs.
- Master the technical specifications for producing books to avoid delays during the publication process. Know the trim size, have correct margins, ensure that fonts are embedded, and check that all images are at least 300 dpi.
- Book Cover: People do judge a book by its cover. Look at best-selling books in and across your niche for inspiration. I would recommend collaborating with a qualified designer during this process. Covers for printed books and e-covers are slightly different.
  - Printed books: front cover, spine, and back cover
  - Resolution should be 300 DPI
  - JPEG or TIFF files only
  - Need to know the trim size. Avoid too big or too small and instead aim *roughly* around the industry's norm
  - If your book contains excessive images, then you may want to consider page bleed. To calculate the dimensions of a black and white book with bleed, take the trim size and use one of the following formulas:
  - bleed height = bleed + height + bleed   bleed width = bleed + height
  - The numerical value of the *bleed* equals ⅛ inch, or 0.125". Therefore, for a 6 x 9" book, the dimensions with bleed will be 6.125 x 9.25."

- The barcode should be in a 2 x 1.2" white box in the lower right hand corner of the book.
- For e-book cover details:
    - KDP accepts two types of files for cover images in RBG color format
        - JPEG (JPEG/JPG)
        - TIFF(TIF/TIFF)
        - Ideal dimensions are 2,560 x 1,600 pixels, minimum image size is 1,000 x 625, and maximum image size allowed is 10,000 x 10,000
        - Cover image must be less than 50MB, minimum resolution of 300 PPI (pixels- per-inch)
        - To upload an e-book cover to Amazon KDP, you must upload just the front cover only. E-books don't have barcodes.

CHAPTER IV:
E-book distribution & Print on Demand

Your book is not officially published until it's made available to the public. Authors can distribute their books through e-book distribution services, or authors can distribute their physical books to traditional brick-and-mortar businesses like bookstores.

The first part of this chapter concentrates on the ways that webmasters can electronically distribute their books. Amazon KDP is a mega-popular platform, but there are also dark horses in the e-book distribution business, such as Smashwords and Kobo. I'll reveal various outlets that you can use to print your book on demand. The popular solution is CreateSpace, but depending on the type of book you're trying to create, it's worth considering other POD services. I list some of the most popular ones and break them down so that self-publishers will be equipped with an arsenal of options.

Amazon Kindle Direct Publishing (KDP)

Amazon KDP is the mecca for when it comes to e-book publishing. It has a customer base that reaches millions of readers and is the go-to place for first time e-book publishers.

There are many resources available that describe how to make your e-book available on the KDP marketplace. You can learn how to do this by reading the KDP Jumpstart article.[1]

But first things first, authors should have a solid understanding about the book publishing business. So, let's talk about money! There are two royalty options in KDP, which are 35% and 70% royalties.[2]

Now, the latter clearly sounds like the better choice of the two, but there are three stipulations to get the larger share of commissions. If you choose the standard royalty option for e-books, or 35%, then there are three price range requirements: if the file is less than 3 megabytes, it must be priced within $0.99-$200; if it's greater than or equal to 3 megabytes and less than 10 megabytes, it must be priced within the range of $1.99-$200; and if it's 10 megabytes or greater, then it must fall within the range of $2.99-$200. Therefore, it's always a good idea to make sure your e-book is coded cleanly to optimize file size. Including many images in your e-book will make it "heavy." To learn how to optimize your e-book, check out the "Reduce Your Ebook Manuscript File Size"[3] article. To be eligible for 70% commission, the price of your e-book must fall within the range of $2.99-$9.99. [2]

- 70% royalty options are only available for select countries. To see the list of countries eligible read about Ebook Royalty Options.[4]
- To earn 70% royalty on sales to customers in Brazil, Japan, Mexico, and India, you must be enrolled in the KDP Select program and meet the 70% list price requirements.

Let's say that the list price for an e-book is $9.99, with a royalty of 70% commission, 1 MB size, and a customer whose applicable Value-Added Tax (VAT) rate is 0%. The formula for calculating the royalty is as follows:

Royalty = Royalty Rate x (List Price - Delivery Cost - Applicable VAT)

In this case plugging the numbers into the formula will look like this:
- Royalty = .70 x ($9.99 - $0.15 - $0.00)
- Royalty = $6.88

Linking a physical book with e-book: If you offer a physical version of your book (highly recommended) then it's a good idea to make sure that it's linked with your e-book. This ensures that prospective readers will see both book editions in one setting and have more options. This is great because some people don't mind reading e-books on a screen while others solely prefer the classic paper book. All you have to do is enter the exact details of your physical book in KDP and Amazon will attempt to sync it for you. The details you need to enter are: title and subtitle, author and contributor, volume and edition, and language. If you have a paperback and e-book of the same title and all the information is an exact match, then Amazon will automatically link these together for you. To learn more, read the article, "Linking Ebook and Paperback Editions."[5]

Smashwords

This is an e-book distribution platform headquartered in the northern Californian town of Los Gatos. The brainchild of former publicist Mark Coker, Smashwords was launched back in 2005. Smashwords has key partnerships with Apple, Barnes & Noble, Kobo, Sony, and hopefully you in the future.

There are three primary catalogs in which you can list your book in for Smashwords: Premium, Standard, and Atom/OPDS. The catalog that I would recommend focusing on is Premium as it gives you a higher range of distribution. Once you get listed in the premium catalog, your book will also be distributed to the following:

- Apple (iBooks)
- Barnes & Noble
- Scribd
- Kobo
- Blio
- Inktera
- OverDrive
- Baker and Taylor (Axis 360)
- Gardners (UK)

It's important to note that even though Smashbooks has a distribution agreement with Amazon, there's still a possibility that your e-book will not be synced with Amazon KDP. The reason for this is Amazon's inability to receive Smashwords' entire catalog—however, if your book earned at least $2,000 with Smashwords retailers, and if you wish for Smashwords to sync your book to Amazon KDP, then you can contact Smashwords support to let them know that you're in the $2,000 club. My advice is to simply create your own listing on Amazon KDP as it's a free, simple process guaranteeing your inclusion in Amazon.

To gain traction in Smashwords, make sure your title is included in the premium catalog. Smashwords, like any respectable e-book distribution service, simply wants the best quality e-books in their catalog. In order for them to do this, e-books uploaded to Smashwords need to match the mechanical requirements of their distribution partners. According to Smashwords, an e-book simply meeting mechanical requirements doesn't mean that it reflects the quality of content or marketability of the e-book.[6] Instead, it simply means that the book is produced in a high-quality manner. Things like cover, formatting, and layout should be similar to that of books published under a Big 5 Publisher.

It's important to understand how books are evaluated for inclusion in the premium catalog. All e-books go through a two-step vetting process. Step one is automated and step two is manual. In step one, a program called "AutoVetter" checks to ensure that the submitted EPUB adheres to the Smashwords style guide. In step two, the EPUB file is manually inspected by a human to see if there's something that AutoVetter missed out on, which typically takes a couple of business days.

You're allowed to make changes to your book after it passes inspection. The wait time for the second go around will typically be shorter. If you have an inquisitive mind, then you can read the Smashwords Style Guide.[7] This is not something that's read in one sitting as it's 117 pages long. Here's a quick checklist of things to keep in mind to produce an e-book that satisfies the Smashwords style guide:

- Make sure you submit an EPUB file. It's recommended to ensure that your file passes EpubCheck.[8]
- Book title: make sure that your title matches exactly the one that's on the book cover. Avoid adding extra words.
- Book cover: make sure that it's of professional quality. In other words, if your book cover was juxtaposed next to a bestseller in your genre, your book cover would look similar in quality. Smashwords accepts JPG or PNG files.[9] Only the front cover is needed for e-books. A full cover, or one with a back cover and spine, is only needed for printed books.
    - Cover should include title and author name.
    - Ideal cover is vertical and 1600 pixels wide, 2400 tall, and with a minimum width of 1400 pixels.
    - Must have a copyright page which states the author as the copyright holder. An example of such a page is listed below:

There are some arguments in online self-publishing forums that Smashwords content guidelines are too strict and demanding. My motto is that if you can pass the strictest guidelines, then everything else will be smooth sailing.

Kobo

Founded in December 2009, Kobo is a Toronto-based company that provides e-reading services and e-reading devices. If you're curious, "kobo" is a word concocted by re-arranging the letters of the word, "book." Kobo is sometimes touted as the last true competitor of Amazon in the e-reading market.[10] Perhaps a reason for this is due to their global key partnerships with brick and mortar businesses. One of the advantages of distributing your e-book through Kobo is your e-book can be made available in all partner countries through their websites.[11] This is critical for authors who wish to reach a global audience.

The good news about prepping your e-book for places like Amazon KDP and Smashwords is you'll quickly become familiar with the e-book publication process. All you need to publish through Kobo is a .jpeg or .png file for the e-cover, and an .epub or .pdf file for the manuscript. You'll then need to enter your credit card details so that you can get paid.[12] Kobo will make payments to publishers and provide reporting details within 45 days following the end of the applicable month. Kobo may accrue and hold payments due until the total amount is $100.[13] To get started with publishing on Kobo, follow the steps by visiting their site.[14]

Print on Demand (POD) Services

It goes without saying, but to produce a physical copy of your book, you need to get it printed. One of the simplest ways to do this is by using a print-on-demand (POD) service. After everything is set up, copies will only be printed and shipped when an order is placed. This entire process is all hands-free.

There are several popular POD services available. In this section I'll provide an overview of each one, and then towards the end of the chapter, I'll provide a fictional example to give you a better idea of how the POD process works.

CreateSpace: This company was originally launched back in 2000 under the name of BookSurge. It was started by a coalition of writers whose goal was to create a publishing platform for writers. They wanted authors to retain more control over the rights of their work and profits. In 2002, Custom-Flix Labs was started by four colleagues who wanted to make it easier for independent filmmakers to distribute their creative work. In 2005, Amazon acquired both companies, and fast forward to the present, they're now combined under the CreateSpace (CS) brand. Even though CS is primarily known as a POD company, it also provides content creators the ability to sell CDs and DVDs on demand. CreateSpace is known for offering some of the best royalties in the industry along with having excellent customer service. There's no setup fees involved to get started, and to setup your title, all you must do is follow the instructions on their website.[15]

Some of the key options you should pay attention to when considering a POD service are royalties, printing options, and distribution. It's said that CS has some of the best payouts in the industry, but let's get more specific.

Let's assume that a Mr. Z is venturing into the wild world of self-publishing. Mr. Z recently finished a 220-page memoir about his life as a circus performer. The memoir goes through all phases of his life and in each one, he includes several photos so that the reader can see his progression throughout life in a more candid manner. He decides to go with a black and white 5 x 8" trim on white paper. He chooses black and white as opposed to color in order to reduce printing costs. He decides that the price of his story should be $12.95. With these details, after each sale through Amazon using CreateSpace as the POD service, his royalty will be $4.28. If it was done through expanded distribution, the royalty would be $1.69. This number was calculated by using the CreateSpace Book Royalty Calculator.[16]

For books sold through Amazon standard distribution, they'll take 40% of the sales and 60% for expanded distribution. Examples of sales that occur through Expanded Distribution are from bookstores, online retailers, libraries, and academic institutions. If you use your own ISBN, then your book is not eligible for the libraries and academic portions of expanded distribution. It can still, however, be eligible for bookstore and online retailers.[17]

In addition to Amazon's distribution fees, you'll have to take into account the cost for manufacturing the book. It's a flat $2.15 per book with 24-108 pages, and for books in the range of 110-828 pages, it's a flat fee of $0.85. You might be thinking, "What gives? How can a book with more pages have a lower

Distribution fee?" Well, it's not actually lower. Books within the 110-828 page range are also charged $.012 per page while the ones that fall within the 24-108 page range aren't charged anything additional. For a full-colored book, it's a flat $3.65 per 24-40 pages and with books 42-500 pages, it's a flat $0.85 per book. For full colored books 24-40 pages, there's no print-per-page fee, but for colored books 42-500 pages, it costs $0.07 per page.

Since it's good business to understand how all of this works, let's do some simple math by hand to see if our numbers match up with the CreateSpace calculator. Let's assume that we have a book with the following details:

• List price: $12.95
• Number of pages: 220
• Standard distribution
• Interior pages: black & white

The formula that's used to calculate royalties for books sold via standard distribution, with black & white pages, and within the 110-828 page range is listed below:

Royalty = List Price - (.40 x List Price + $0.85 + $0.012 x Number of Pages)

Here's how the computation will look after plugging in the numbers: Royalty = $12.95 - ($5.18 + $0.85 + $2.64) = $4.28

If the book has less than 110 pages or if the book uses colored pages, then the formula needs to be modified. Let's assume that Mr. Z wants to now consider printing his book in color and see what his royalty would be like via standard distribution. The formula would be modified as follows:

Royalty = List Price - (.40 x List Price + $0.85 + $0.07 x Number of Pages)
Royalty = $12.95 - ($5.18 + $0.85 + $0.07 x 220) = -$8.48

Ouch, that's not good business to lose money with each sale! If you investigate the two formulas, there's just one difference which is the cost to print per page. With black and white, it's $0.012 per page, and with color printing it's $0.07 per page. The cost to print-per-page is what runs the cost of printing up when you're dealing with color printing. There's not much you can do in this case as printing full colored books are expensive regardless of which POD service you use. That's why it's a good idea to become familiar with these formulas as it will give you a rough idea on what page range your book should be in. It would be a travesty if you spent months working on a full colored book only to find out that it's too expensive to self-publish via POD. It's generally a better idea to keep the page count on the smaller scale with colored POD books. An example of a genre in which the page counts are normally on the smaller side are children's books—roughly 32 pages—which means better royalties for self-published authors.

Lightning Source (Ingram): To set the record straight, Lightning Source and IngramSpark are subsidiaries of the Ingram Content Group (ICG), headquartered in La Vergne, Tennessee. ICG is one of America's largest book distributors with access to over 7.5 million titles. The primary markets that ICG targets are librarians, booksellers, and educators. Therefore, if you want your book to be distributed to any of these markets, then ICG is worth a consideration. Lightning Source is a business unit in ICG, also located in La Vergne, Tennessee, and its specialty is print-on-demand.

The difference between IngramSpark and Lightning Source is kind of confusing. Ever since the year 1997, ICG has been helping publishers bring their books to market with POD technology. As mentioned previously, Lightning Source is the POD unit of ICG, while IngramSpark is the combination of Lightning Source POD technology with CoreSource®, which is ICG's e-book distribution platform. Both IS and LS provide the same trim sizes and binding types without any added printing costs, and they both allow for flexible ranges of trade discounts on titles. Compared to CreateSpace, IngramSpark offers additional cover options like hardcover, saddle stitch binding, along with two color options: standard color, which is the economical plan, and premium color. They also offer more trim sizes. Learn how to create your accounts with IngramSpark[18] and Lightning Source.[19]

Lulu: This is a print-on-demand company headquartered in Morrisville, North Carolina. The company was founded by Canadian entrepreneur Robert

Young who also co-founded Red Hat. The three main distinctions between Lulu and CreateSpace are printing costs, printing options, and publishing selections. At the time of publication, Lulu provides the option for publishers to print hardcover books, and they also enable e-book distribution. When it comes to printing paperbacks, Lulu is more expensive than CreateSpace. You can learn more about the printing costs in Lulu by reading the "How much will my printed book cost?"[20] article on their site. To learn the steps on how to get started publishing with Lulu, visit their homepage.[21]

Blurb: This is a self-publishing platform based in San Francisco, California that was founded by Eileen Gittins in 2005. Like CreateSpace and Lulu, Blurb provides print-on-demand options and like Lulu, Blurb offers hardcover printing. For e-books, you have the option of submitting a fixed-layout e-book, reflowable e-book, or pdf. Blurb also provides publishers with online sale tools to help them facilitate the marketing process. For example, it includes options to integrate your book with the Kickstarter's crowdfunding site or to share a preview of your project on social media sites. Popular types of books sold on Blurb are cookbooks, photography, memoirs, children's books, novels, and poetry. To get started selling with Blurb, you can read their Sell & Distribute page.[22]

I'm still confused!

Okay, so you just received a buffet of print-on-demand services you can use for your book. However, if you're a first-time self-publisher, then all of this may seem a bit overwhelming. That's natural because writing is difficult, editing is meticulous, and publishing is hair-pulling. Yikes!

So which print-on-demand service should you use? It completely depends on your priorities and what you're trying to accomplish. A couple of elements that may factor into your decision is what type of book you want, if it's mandatory that your book is in color, your financial goals, and if retail stores will be part of your marketing plan. Fear not, as this section will hopefully provide entertaining examples to help paint a better picture for you on which path to take.

Sally's Plan: Let's assume that "Sally Sue" is a first-time novelist hailing from beautiful Portland, Oregon, United States. She finished her debut novel—a dystopia in which the protagonist has to figure out how to restore order to the world and the odds are clearly stacked against her. She finished the novel which is 370 pages and she's thinking of the following details: 6 x 9", black and white, hardback binding cloth blue, cream page, and gloss lamination. Since she's an avid collector of hardcover books, it's imperative that there's a hardcover edition of her book available. The quality of print is very important to her as the novel contains some character sketches, so she's willing to take a cut in profit in order to put the best quality product in the hands of her customers. Her rationale is that she plans on releasing two more follow-up books, and the first installment of the series is just to build brand name recognition. Which POD service should Sally Sue use and why?

Well, let's analyze a couple of things. A hardcover book is the version of a book with a thicker cover to make it more durable than its paperback variant. It's also commonly enveloped with a dust jacket. If a book is anticipated to generate many sales, then a hardcover edition is typically released before the paperback version. In the past, hardback books were typically released a year before the paperback edition, but in recent years it has been released roughly six months in advance. Hardback books are typically only printed for books that are expected to sell well, such as books written by authors with cult-followings like J.K. Rowling. Even though Sally is no J.K. Rowling, she loves hardcover books herself and decides that a hardcover book is a must strictly for personal reasons. In this case, the POD services Sally needs to pay attention to are Blurb, Lulu, and IngramSpark. At the time of publication, CreateSpace doesn't offer POD services for hardcover books as their specialty is affordable paperbacks. Therefore, Sally options are mainly IngramSpark, Lulu, and Blurb.

Let's look at IngramSpark. There are many fees a first-time author should be aware of. There's a $49 setup fee,[23] a $12 yearly fee (also known as their market access fee)[24] and a $25 file revision fee.[25] The $12 yearly fee may seem annoying, but this does enable availability to 39,000 retailers and libraries including Barnes & Noble and indie bookstores. Also, your title will get a detailed listing in the daily catalogs that Lightning Source provides to all its U.S. distribution partners, such as Baker & Taylor.

The revision fee is unattractive, but you can minimize your chances of having your title flagged by thoroughly reading through the file requirements section for print files[26] and EPUBs[27] in IngramSpark. You can also get the $49 setup fee refunded if you print an order of 50 or more books within 60 days.[23] It's not a bad idea for authors to have physical copies of their books to give away for reviews and sell at speaking events. Additionally, if gaining distribution to retail outlets and libraries is critical to your marketing plan, then IngramSpark is the "spark" you'll need for this as its one of the largest distributors in the United States. It helps that the print quality of IngramSpark is generally considered amongst the highest in the industry.

Going back to Sally's example, let's assume she wants to discover the cost to print her 370-page, 6 x 9", black & white, hardback binding cloth blue, cream page book with gloss lamination. Going off these details, it will cost Sally a total of $17.49 to print and ship a single copy of this book. This also excludes the trade discount, or the discount that Sally would have to provide retailers in order for her book to be stocked on their shelves. This would be a total discount of 55%; 40% is the industry's standard discount for books and 15% is for Ingram's cut.

So off the bat, Sally loses 55% of her profits, and then the costs to manufacture the book must also be accounted for. Therefore, if Sally provides a retail price of $19.99 and offers a trade discount of 55%, then her net profit off one book will be $0.29. The costs were calculated using IngramSpark Publisher Compensation Calculator.[28] To further increase her chances of retailers stocking her books, she needs to make her book returnable. This is an industry standard and Sally will be charged the wholesale price if a return is made.

Sally is a little disgruntled by the amount of profit she'll make if she sells her book to retail stores. She rethinks things over and decides to tweak her original plan. Since making the hardcover option available is very important to her, she's going to move forward with it. She also doesn't want to increase the retail price of the book as she wants the hardcover book to be below the average market price for hardcover books in her genre. She feels that this will make it easier for her to gain traction as a new author. After six months, she plans to release the paperback version of the book at $14.95. The amount of money she'll make per sale with the paperback edition using Ingram as the distributor will be $1.06.

Still not inspiring, but it's close to quadruple the profit she'll make from the hardcover version. After reading various articles online, Sally decides that when she releases the paperback edition, she will instead use CreateSpace as the POD service. She feels like the quality of a printed black and white paperback between these services will be negligible and she wants to make a larger profit. If she priced her paperback at $14.95 and sold it on Amazon via CreateSpace, then her royalty would be $3.68.

After reading the Amazon KDP forum, Sally realizes that her best bet to make larger profits is to offer a Kindle version of her book and focus most of her attention on driving online sales. She plans to list her e-book at $9.99 and opt in for the 70% commission structure so that she'll make $6.88 per sale. She finalizes her marketing plan and knows that she will initially launch the hardcover and e-book version of her book priced $19.99 and $9.99, respectively. She plans to optimize her Amazon listing to drive e-book sales, host book signings, and make public appearances so that she can drive sales of her hardcover books.

After six months of hard promotion, she will release the paperback version of her book through CreateSpace.

Now that Sally has a good idea of the profit she'll make from the hardcover, paperback, and electronic format of her books, she can start thinking about what income goals she can realistically reach.

Analysis: When you step into the world of publishing, you're no longer just an author, you're also an infopreneur. You must understand the entire process involved when taking your creativity and wrapping it into a book. When you're creating a physical product, you need to understand all the manufacturing costs, all parties involved, and the business of how book stores operate. I can't stress enough the importance for authors to create a marketing plan for their book and do some business math. With the popularity of POD services, there's no reason why an author shouldn't make their book available in physical format. This will provide prospective readers more options and increase the self-publisher's marketing opportunities.

They won't be limited to just e-book distributors, but will also be granted the opportunity of having their brain child distributed to thousands of brick-and-mortar stores. In Sally Sue's case, she wants to offer multiple physical versions of her work. This means that Sally must also have a unique ISBN number for each book edition, and that she must also understand how to appropriately price each one. Pricing too high above the industry's average runs the risk of her making few sales, and pricing too low means that her profits will be close to nothing. Sally realizes that she will not generate much income with her hardcover book, but she instead wants to look forward and competitively price it in the hopes of generating more sales and producing a popular book. This will allow her future books to generate more sales and potentially more opportunities.

Bookstores are a business, and business dictates that you sell whatever book there's a strong demand for. If sales for Sally's flagship book go well in retailers, then when the sequel comes out, retailers will have no problem ordering copies. It's good business for them to do so as Sally is now a vetted author.

Many things are involved in the sale of a book. The author must come up with the idea and use their skills to create a polished product. Next, the author must find a way to manufacture and print the product which incurs a cost. Then, the author may decide to have their book sold at a retail store who typically purchases through wholesalers at a discount. In order for bookstores to remain in business in a hyper-competitive landscape, they must be selective with which books they choose to stock on their shelves. They must only stock books that sell or they won't remain in business. The author, publisher, distributor, wholesaler and retailer are all working together.

While Sally realizes she must be forward thinking, she also knows that she needs to generate profit in order to make it practical for her to stay in the book business. She decides that it makes sense to focus the majority of her efforts on promoting the e-book version of her book due to higher profit margins, and then six months following the release of her hardcover book, she can then release the paperback version. She can price it lower than the hardcover edition and make higher profits through Amazon if she uses CreateSpace. She decides to use two POD companies as using IngramSpark gives her the opportunity to make her hardcover book available on POD with the addition of access to many distributors—she also plans on using CreateSpace so that she can yield higher profit margins with her paperback edition sold on Amazon. One of the benefits of being a hybrid author/publisher is that you have the authority to make these decisions. There's nothing stopping you from utilizing more than one print-on-demand service.

CHAPTER V:
Tactical Amazon Promotion

Amazon is a mammoth internet retailer that was started in humble beginnings by founder and still current CEO Jeff Bezos. Amazon is the main player when it comes to self-publishing with their Kindle Direct Publishing (KDP) service. This makes it convenient for writers to self-publish their e-books, and with their subsidiary company CreateSpace, authors can print their books on demand in a hassle-free, hands-off manner. Amazon also provides several promotional opportunities for authors, which will be discussed in detail later in this chapter. All of these opportunities should be thoroughly analyzed so that authors can decide if it will make sense to incorporate them within their marketing mix.

Amazon Marketing Services (AMS)

Amazon has millions of dedicated book readers who purchased from their extensive catalog. With so many readers in their customer database, it makes sense for them to offer an advertising solution to help authors get more eyeballs on their Amazon page description. Let's face it, there can only be one book that ranks number one in Amazon for a specific category. Therefore, what happens to all the other quality books that are drowned in the crowd of Amazon listings? The answer is that they'll likely not see the light of day. Therefore, authors in this predicament may want to consider purchasing ads on AMS to generate more sales. Here are some of the benefits of getting started with AMS:

- **Pay per click mode:** Similar to AdWords, AMS uses a pay-per-click Model, meaning that the seller will only be charged when a prospect clicks on their ad.

- **Auction based system:** Like AdWords, sellers can "bid" on keywords so that they'll never pay more than a certain amount per click.
- **Can manage your budget:** Sellers can set the maximum budget for a campaign, and can start or stop it when they desire. Sellers must pay a minimum of $1.00 per day to have their campaigns eligible to run.
- **Manual or automatic keyword selection:** You can manually set the keywords you want your ad to show up under, or you can allow Amazon to automatically select the keywords that match your product.
- **Control campaign duration:** Can let the ad run continuously or set the date range in which the ad runs.
- **Detailed analytics:** Can get keyword and campaign level sales reporting.

You can learn more by reading the Frequently Asked Questions on AMS Sponsored Products and Product Display Ads.[1] Getting started with AMS is simple. You must first have an Amazon KDP account setup with an active title. Once completed, the next step is to run an ad for your desired title. You can do this by finding the title in your KDP bookshelf, and then click on the "Promote and Advertise" button under the text: E-BOOK KINDLE ACTIONS. You'll then be directed to a page that provides you four options. The one that you want to concentrate on is with the text, "Run an Ad Campaign." It has a yellow button that says: "Accept and create an ad campaign."

Bear in mind that when you click on the button, you're agreeing to create an Amazon Marketing Services (AMS) account and are therefore subject to the Amazon Marketing Services Agreement.[2] Once selected you'll be redirected to choose a campaign type. You'll have the option of choosing Sponsored Products or Product Display Ads.

Sponsored product ads: Keyword-targeted ads that show up in the Amazon search results and on product detail pages. Can be used to promote new re-leases or older titles and is great for increasing search presence.

Product Display ads: Delivers ads on the product pages of related products or based on shoppers' interest. The "Sponsored Products: How to Get Started Tutorial"[3] is an instructive video from Amazon Marketing Services that explains how sponsored product ads work, and the "Getting Started with

Product Display Ads"[4] video shows how product display ads work. Once you select which campaign type to use, follow the remaining steps to get your first ad up and running.

Select a book to advertise: If you have more than one book published in KDP, then make sure you select the correct one. If the default selection is not correct, click the gray "Change" button.

Set your campaign name, budget, and duration: Enter your campaign name, average daily budget, and duration. The minimum daily budget is $1.00.

Select a targeting type: This refers to keywords that will trigger the display of your ads. You have the option of automatic or manual targeting. With automatic targeting, Amazon analyzes your product details and decides which keywords will trigger the display of your ads. With manual targeting, you choose which keywords will trigger the display of your ads. You'll also decide the keywords match type—these are parameters that modify the display of your ads.

Amazon allows three match types which are: broad, phrase, and exact. With broad keywords, your ad will appear as long as the keywords you define are used in a search query. For a phrase keyword, your ad will appear if someone searches for your keyword in its exact order with any text before or after it. With exact match, your ad will display when someone searches for your exact keyword phrase. For example, let's imagine that the keyword phrase you want to target is *bluetooth smartwatch*. Here are the search queries that will cause the ad to render under each circumstance:

- Broad: bluetooth smartwatch with camera
- Phrase: digital bluetooth smartwatch
- Exact: bluetooth smartwatch

Once you figured out which targeting type to use, you can enter the cost- per-click bid. The general rule of thumb is to enter the price that you're absolutely comfortable paying per click. The lowest number you can enter for each keyword is $0.02. The next portion that you'll want to fill out is the text that will display when your ad is shown. You'll have a maximum of 150 characters to use so make the most of this "digital real-estate." Once that's done, the only steps remaining is for you to enter your payment credentials and wait for your campaign approval.

Some basic metrics you'll want to monitor are impressions, click through rate (CTR), and sales. *Impressions* refers to how many times your ad was displayed, and *CTR* refers to how many times your ad was clicked on. You'll want to increase both the impressions and the percentage of the CTR. Doing so means that your ad will be displayed more often and the CTR means that your book description will be seen.

Once you're able to generate enough impressions and a high click through, the tell-tale metric in determining the success of your campaign is the amount of sales it generates. Amazon Marketing Services recommends starting off using automatic targeting, and then after two weeks, download your keyword performance report and analyze which keywords generate the most impressions, CTRs, and sales. You can then modify your campaign settings to use manual targeting if you prefer.

This method will provide you with verifiable proof on which keywords produce the best results, so it makes sense to increase the bid on these keywords so that you can pour more money on the ones that are producing the best results. From here on, you keep monitoring the campaigns and making the appropriate adjustments when needed. Good news for us, Amazon provides a plethora of information we can use to take your marketing efforts to the next level. For more tips on how to advertise your e-book with Amazon read "Advertising for KDP Ebooks."[5]

Know your numbers: Depending on the stage of your business, investing in AMS may not make sense. For example, if a writer created an e-book that's priced at $0.99, then it may not be economical to invest in AMS because the amount they'll need to spend to acquire a new reader may result in a negative balance. In this case, it's better for them to wait until they have created a series and have several books published under their name. This way, when readers see their ad and purchase one of their books, they will have the opportunity to purchase the other books in the series, allowing the writer to accumulate more sales from a single advertising effort, stretching the value of their advertising dollar.

KDP Select

To join KDP Select,[6] your book MUST be exclusive to the Kindle Store. In other words, you can't sell your e-book outside of the Kindle marketplace, and you can't give away any free copies of the book. You're not even allowed to sell the e-book from your site. This contingency is valid for as long as your book is enrolled in KDP Select. Once the time period has elapsed, the exclusivity clause is revoked and the power to do what you want with the e-book is transferred back to you:

- If you make your book available to KDP Select, your book will be included in Kindle Unlimited (KU) and Kindle Owners' Lending Library (KOLL). In addition, you can earn a portion of the KDP Select Global Fund.

- Enrolling in the KDP Select program provides you access to additional tools. You'll be able to use time sensitive countdowns and free book promotion in which readers can obtain access to your book for free for a limited time.

- Enrolling in the KDP Select program is only available to those who have published their own book. For example, authors that are going the traditional route of using a publisher will not qualify.

Kindle Unlimited & Kindle Owners' Lending Library (KOLL): Kindle Unlimited[7] is a subscription-based program for book junkies. For the cost of $9.99 a month, subscribers gain access to over one million titles, thousands of audiobooks, and even the latest magazines. If you enroll in KDP Select, your book will be available for free via Kindle Unlimited. This is smart business for Amazon as they can provide their subscribers with additional content off the efforts of various authors. You can enroll a single book, just one of your books, or all your books into KOLL.

Authors enrolled in KDP select are eligible for 70% royalty for sales in Brazil, India, Japan, and Mexico. The Kindle Owners' Library[8] is a program available to Amazon Prime members who have a Kindle device. This feature allows them to choose a book to borrow with no due dates. It's like a digital equivalent to a physical library, except you're limited to "borrowing" one book a month the due date for the book can be as long as you want. If you do decide to enroll in KDP Select, then you might as well use the tools that Amazon makes available.

Kindle Countdown Deals: This is a feature available to all authors enrolled in KDP Select. It allows authors the ability to set limited time discounts for their e-books. When a prospect views your book description, they'll see:

product description, original price of the book, the discount price, and a countdown clock revealing how much time is left before the price increments. To learn how to create a new countdown, read "Adding a Kindle Countdown Deal."[9]

One perk of Kindle Countdowns is that you'll still receive the royalty percentage you originally signed up for even during the countdown period. For example, if you signed up for 70% royalties, then you'll still receive it even if you drop the price of the e-book below $2.99.

Here's an example of how a Kindle Countdown deal works. The book has a list price of $3.99. You start the promotion on Tuesday at 9:00 a.m., discounted to $0.99 with a price increment of $1.00 every 24 hours:

- Wednesday at 9:00 a.m., price jumps to $1.99
- Thursday at 9:00 a.m., price jumps to $2.99
- Friday at 9:00 a.m., price jumps to $3.99

There's a dedicated website for active Kindle Countdown Deals if you would like to see some live examples.[10]

Before you create your countdown deal, it's worth having a strategy. Yes, a lower price tends to lead to higher conversions, but you still need to put work in to get eyeballs on your offer. Don't forget about your social media assets such as Facebook, Twitter, Instagram, and LinkedIn. Everyone likes a good deal, and by offering it to your followers, you will help establish rapport with them.

Free book promotion: Another tool made available by KDP Select is the Free Book Promotions. You can run a free book promo for up to five days every 90-day enrollment period. Since your e-book will be free during this time period, you'll not be eligible for any royalties. However, the free promo can help get your e-book in front of the eyes of more readers and thus increase your reviews, which could lead to future sales.

Once you enroll your book into the free KDP promo, you should know that your e-book will automatically be transferred from the top paid products to the top free ones in the Kindle Store. Sales rank is the combination of your cur- rent sales and your overall sales history with more weight attributed to the recent sales. When the free period is over, the book's previous paid rank will influence its new ranking.[11]

How you structure the free day period is entirely up to you. You don't have to continuously run your offer for five days. You can mix up the duration, such as offering it every other day or for a couple of consecutive days. To learn more about how to do free book promos, you can read the "Free Book Promotions"[12] article.

Should you use Kindle Select? Let's do a quick recap of all the services that Amazon provides because there are quite a few funny acronyms to re- member. There are a couple of programs available in Kindle, which are the Kindle Owners' Lending Library (KOLL) and Kindle Unlimited (KU). These are two subscription-based programs that make Kindle titles available to readers. The primary difference between KOLL and KU is that KU has a separate standalone subscription program while Amazon customers are eligible for KOLL if they have a prime membership. At this time, for $9.99 per month, KU allows readers to download and read an unlimited number of e-books on their Kindle device, while KOLL readers are limited to borrowing one e-book a month.

Now that we got some of the jargon out of the way, it's time to answer the question: to be or not to be with KDP Select? It's actually a simple answer. Are you comfortable with relinquishing control over your product or do you prefer to keep full control and execute your own marketing plan? Only you can truly answer that.

Kindle Matchbook

Many authors offer a physical edition of their book which is something I highly encourage. However, authors can increase their overall revenue if they also offer a discounted version of their e-book to customers who purchased the paperback counterpart. It makes good business sense because a customer who purchased a paperback version of your book may also be interested in downloading the e-book edition. Having both editions provides them more flexibility as they will not only have a physical copy that they can hold, but they'll also have a portable, multi-platform book edition. Readers don't need to own a Kindle device to read e-books available in the Kindle Store. They can download the Kindle Reader app[13] on their smartphone and read away.

Amazon Gifting

Want to provide your e-book as a gift to some of your favorite people? Go ahead and share the love! Doing so could increase the chances of getting your book reviewed. Gifting is an incredible tool to help you grow awareness of your book. Bonus: gifts don't expire. When you gift your e-book, the recipient isn't obligated to redeem the gift. After all, gifts are meant to be given with no strings attached. The recipient can choose to:

- Accept your gift by redeeming the card
- Choose to exchange it for an Amazon gift card of equal value

If the person you're trying to gift is located in a country where this option is not available, then sadly you won't be able to gift your e-book to them. Instead, Amazon recommends you purchase a gift card with the exact value of your e-book, and suggest they use the card to purchase your e-book.

To learn how to provide your e-book as a gift, read the article, "Purchase a Kindle Book as a Gift."[14]

Kindle Pre-order

KDP gives you the ability to make your e-book available for pre-order up to 90 days before the launch of your e-book. Customers will be able to pre-order it any time before the launch date, and on the scheduled release their e-book will become available. This allows authors the advantage of getting their book details public so that they can start promoting it.

I like to think of a marketing campaign in terms of morning, afternoon, and evening. You should do promotion before the book is out, so that you can start building awareness; once the book is launched, you continue executing your marketing, and well after the book is released, you should fine tune the marketing campaign.

Once your e-book pre-order is properly setup, a timer will be displayed on your book description page showing how much time is left until your book is officially released. To follow the exact steps you'll need to take to make your e-book available for pre-order, read the article "Kindle E-book Pre-order."[15] Pre-ordering helps contribute to your Amazon sales rank. Once your book is released, the pre-order will be computed into the number. You can keep track of all your pre-order sales in the pre-order report. It will include useful marketing data, such as pre-ordered units, pre-ordered cancellations, and net pre-orders. Once the pre-order phase is over the sales data will appear in the "others" report.

Things to keep in mind: You can enroll your e-book in KDP Select and still modify the listing during the pre-order period. With KDP Select, customers will receive the content on the scheduled release date. If you make modifications to your listing such as increasing the price, then customers who pre-ordered will retain the price of the original offer. If you reduce the price, then customers will be given a pro-rated refund.

It's important to note that once you list an e-book, you'll need to upload the completed manuscript. Therefore, it's a good idea to wait until you have a final manuscript you're happy with. Amazon will allow you to upload a new manuscript during the pre-order phase, but it will have to be approved again.

However, once you commit to a launch date for your e-book, you should stick to it like glue. Amazon *does* allow pre-order campaigns to be canceled but not without penalty. If the preorder is canceled, then customers will be properly refunded and you'll be disallowed from listing any e-book on pre-order for a year. So, think carefully before setting up a pre-order campaign without doing your homework first.

Amazon book descriptions

Your Amazon book description is what sells your book to the reader. Without a compelling description, sales will be scarce. One of my favorite tips for writing winning book descriptions is to deeply analyze the top selling books in related genres and take detailed notes about what really stands out in the descriptions and what you feel is missing. To find descriptions of books you can analyze, visit the Amazon homepage and type in the keywords that match your genre. From there, scroll through the results and save the URLs for future reference.

Once you have determined best book description practices for your genre, you can use them as inspiration for putting together a book description of your own. The good thing is that you can always revise your book description. I would recommend continuously editing it so that you can produce the best book description possible. It's important to do this because there's no standardized winning template for producing high-converting book descriptions.

You could also flirt with the idea of hiring an editor from a freelance service like Upwork to edit your book's description. It can be difficult editing your own writing, and sometimes friends and family are too chummy to pro- vide any insightful feedback. However, an unaffiliated third party whose job is to tear your writing into shreds is ironically the person you want. Since book descriptions on Amazon are on the shorter side, it's not going to be costly to get this done.

However, if you prefer to edit on your own, check out Amazon's three tips on writing compelling book descriptions in the article, "KDP Jumpstart Topic 3 - Write Your Book Description."[16] To learn how to format your book descriptions with HTML tags, you can read the article "Supported HTML for Book Description."[17]

At times a book description may not be as important as an appealing book cover and hundreds of glorifying reviews. A beautiful cover, raving reviews, quality product, and compelling description are all ingredients that can help cook up lots of sales.

CHAPTER VI:
Raging Reviews

Reviews are an intricate aspect of the Amazon ecosystem. I personally do plenty of shopping on Amazon and find myself using multiple variables to determine my purchasing decision. I strongly rely on reviews to help assist me with the purchasing process. Smart authors should invest making certain that their reviews are on target. The good news is there are many opportunities for generating reviews. You're going to see how to make the most of them in this chapter.

Editorial Reviews

Contrary to popular belief, Amazon does allow paid reviews, but you have to be careful. The type of paid reviews that Amazon allows are editorial ones which are the type of reviews that have been in existence since the dawn of the publishing industry. Editorial reviews should not appear in the *Customer Review* section of the book listing, but instead in the editorial reviews section, which can be added in Author Central.[1] You can't pay for a favorable review as they must be as unbiased as possible.

Amazon Vine

You may have seen reviews left by customers with the distinctive title of being part of the *Vine Voices* program. Amazon Vine is a group of highly-rated reviewers that get free products. This is a program a person can't just apply for as they're selected based on the number of helpful reviews that they provide. It's kind of like a secret society of sorts, but without all the urban legends. Bear in mind that those who are part of Amazon Vine are not obligated to leave a positive review. Instead, they're encouraged to leave their honest opinions which helps keep the reviews credible. But Amazon Vine might not be the most economical option for newcomers. To learn more about the Amazon Vine program, read the "What is Amazon Vine?" article.[2] If money is not an issue, then here are the steps that vendors can take to make their product eligible for Amazon review.

Create an Amazon Advantage account: This is a consignment program, meaning that the vendor needs to ship their products to the Amazon warehouse, and Amazon then ships your product to customers when they order. You will be paid on a month-by-month basis. Joining this program will put you back $99 yearly. You can read more about Amazon Advantage on the "What is Advantage?" page.[3]

The Big Payback: Once you become eligible for Amazon Advantage, the next step is to pay the fee to become eligible for Amazon Vine. The fee will typically be $2,500 per ASIN. This is excluding the costs to manufacture and ship the books to Amazon.

Top Amazon Reviewers

You can hunt for top Amazon reviewers[4] and try contacting them directly. These reviews will be sorted by rank by default. You can also click on the "Hall of Fame Reviewers"[5] tab to see the top reviewers sorted by this title. Keep in mind that top reviewers are under no obligation to list their contact information. If this is the case, and if the individual doesn't have an online presence, then contacting them outside of Amazon might be difficult. However, if the seller gives vendors the green light to contact them, send your offer. Top reviewers can allow prospective vendors to contact them through the "Send an Email" link on their profile. This can be a time intensive process due to the limited filtering options for top reviewers. In other words, you might need to spend time combing through the results.

Instead of blindly emailing all possible reviewers, developing a strategy would be a more optimal approach. I would recommend analyzing the type of products that they reviewed so you can determine if it's worth both of your time to connect.

Verified vs. Unverified Reviews

There are two types of reviews on Amazon: verified and unverified. Before we go any further, which type of review would you believe is more credible?
1) Verified reviews
2) Unverified reviews

I promise this is not a trick question, but rather an exercise in consumer psychology. The correct answer is choice 1. Verified reviews are definitely the ones I prefer to have as a vendor. That doesn't mean all unverified reviews are not useful because I know from personal experience that this is not the case.

To be precise, an *Amazon Verified Purchase* is one in which Amazon can confirm that the person leaving the review purchased the product on Amazon and didn't receive a deep discount.[6] An unverified review is one in which Amazon can't confirm that it was purchased on Amazon or that the customer paid a price unavailable to most Amazon shoppers. Therefore, if someone purchases your product from eBay and leaves a review for it on Amazon, then it'll display as an unverified review. In this scenario, the reviewer is a legitimate customer, but since it was purchased outside the Amazon environment, it displays as unverified. An article explaining the rules of reviews is titled, "About Customer Reviews,"[7] and is worth a read.

Here are some of the highlights from the article:
- Both favorable and unfavorable reviews are welcome, as long as they're aligned within the spectrum of the community. You can read about the community guidelines from the "Community Guidelines"[8] article.
- Reviews are not to be used to promote or advertise a product. For example, don't review a similar product and then namedrop a product of yours.
- Can't review competitors' products. The reason I suspect this is to avoid conflict of interests.
- Authors can't pay for customer reviews. So "you do this for me, and you're a made man" is not permitted.

- Authors can't review their own products. This rule still holds even if the author discloses his or her identity.
- People living in the same household as the vendor are not allowed to review their product.
- If you find a review inappropriate then below every review there's an option that states, "Was this review helpful to you?" If you select "no," then you'll have the option to tell Amazon a piece of your mind and why the review was not warranted. Amazon may or may not decide to take action on this. However, if you have verifiable proof that it infringes on their community guidelines, then the review is eligible for removal. Amazon lists several examples of the type of reviews that are not allowed on their "Customer Reviews Guidelines Frequently Asked Questions from Authors"[9] article.

To play it safe, authors shouldn't request a review in exchange for anything in return, whether it's monetary or something extra, like bonus content.

Forums

Internet forums have been a focal part of the web for a long time, but with the emergence of social media giants like Facebook, Twitter, YouTube, and Instagram, the popularity of forums is dwindling. However, buried in the back of the web are specialized niche communities, which are not only an excellent opportunity to discover readers that are passionate about a particular topic, but also potential customers for your book as well. Internet forums are still an excellent way to share your expertise, which helps increase your credibility as a sterling professional in your industry.

The primary way to discover forums related to the theme of your book is to simply run appropriate search queries in the search engine of your choice. Forums are also great for finding reviewers as you can search the forum and target users who would be interested in your book.

Before you get started, there are some steps you should follow so that you'll be a good internet citizen. You don't want to be too aggressive as many forums are targeted by spammers and wreaks havoc for forum moderators. Therefore, learn proper forum etiquette before diving headfirst.

Obey the law: You shouldn't just assume that all forums have the same set of rules. That's like assuming all countries have the same laws. Rules vary from forum-to-forum, so it's important to locate the rules and study them before engaging. Typically there will be a "sticky" thread, or a thread that's permanently appended to the top of the forum so that users can read the rules. Make sure to invest time in reading it, and if you have any questions, then message a moderator. It's best to play it safe rather than to make the wrong move and end up getting banned.

Make a better virtual world: As a former forum administrator, I've seen it all. Something that forum owners really hate are drive-by posters, or those who are there for a short period of time in order to maximize their gains at the expense of the forum. Relationships tend to be more meaningful if both parties are benefiting, so discover ways to contribute to the forum and you shall reap the rewards. Some suggestions are to answer questions, engage in discussions, and create resources that forum members will find useful.

Host a book giveaway: Contact the forum administrator and submit your proposal for hosting a free book giveaway. Before you contact the administrator, make sure to analyze the various threads in the forum. Some forums have a thread dedicated to giveaways and contests so it's best to read it so you won't ask questions that have already been answered. Also, some forums may offer advertising you can use to boost the publicity of your contest. This is something that you may want to consider since forum advertising can be a low-investment, high-return endeavor.

Contact specific users: This step requires extreme caution and sharp business acumen. As mentioned previously, forums are high-risk targets for spammers, hackers, scammers, and pretty much any internet criminal you can think of. That's why it's important to build some credibility in the network instead of simply joining and messaging users.

If you followed the previous three steps with little success, then what you can do is target specific members of the forum and present them the opportunity to review your book. This technique is not much different from cold emailing potential reviewers. Search for threads in which users express interest in learning about the topic that your book covers. You can use the search function in the forum to narrow down the time you invest researching. Then, once you find prime candidates, message them offering them the opportunity to review your book. I would not recommend adding a link in the initial message as it may be triggered as spam. Instead, keep it all textual and if they express interest in the book, send them the download link.

YouTube

When I hear authors complain that they've exhausted every single option in scouting reviewers, I politely suggest YouTube. The quick and simple way to find reviewers with YouTube is to visit the homepage, enter keywords related to your book in the search form, and look for YouTube channels that match the theme of your book. You can modify your search query to increase the chances of finding reviewers who will be interested in reviewing your book. It requires nothing diabolical. Just type in the following search query: *keywords + book review + youtube*

For example, if you're writing a book about parenting, then the search query would look like this: *parenting book review youtube*

After watching the video, you can determine if they would be a good candidate for giving reviews. You can send your proposition by clicking on their username, selecting the *ABOUT* tab, and then clicking the comment icon to "Send message." You can read the article in YouTube Help titled, "Send & receive private messages,"[10] for further guidance.

Goodreads

This "social cataloging" site is dedicated to book lovers. It's a good idea for authors to join as there are many promotional opportunities that they can take advantage of. One of the popular ways to promote your book on Goodreads is to host a giveaway contest. In the past, Goodreads only allowed authors to host giveaway contests for published books. This means if you were solely an e-book author, then you were out of luck. However, after continual lobbying by many authors, Goodreads made the right decision and later overturned this ruling, allowing electronic books to be given away. However, there are some stipulations: authors must pay $119, the maximum threshold of e-books to giveaway is 100, and this program is only available to U.S.-based authors.[11] Printed book giveaways are still free for authors to participate in, but they're responsible for eating the shipping and packaging costs. The author can, however, decide which geographic areas are eligible for the offer. For example, if a U.S.-based author is working with a limited budget and doesn't want to ship internationally, then they could just limit participants to the U.S. Below is a strategy on how a new author can maximize their chances for running a successful book promotion contest.

Make it desirable: Don't forget about *AIDA* (attention, interest, desire, action). Anytime there's a lot of content on the web, you'll have to fight hard to standout. Therefore, when you create your free giveaway, it's important to make a post that will captivate the viewer. My advice is to gain inspiration from other Goodreads giveaway contests and add your own "spice" to it. You can see examples of this by visiting the Giveaway[12] portion of their site.

Speedy follow-up: If you're offering a printed book, then make sure to ship it in a timely fashion. The last thing you want is for the contest winner to think that you didn't live up to your promise. It's possible to get bad reviews because of this! Goodreads will provide you with the shipping information of the winner so make sure to mark your calendar and know when your contest ends. To be extra prepared, you can have all the items needed to ship the package, such as a bubble envelope and shipping labels. The location of the contest winner will be unveiled once the contest ends. You can read the terms and conditions about hosting Goodreads contests by reading the Giveaway Terms & Conditions.[13]

Personalize the gift: It never hurts to go the extra mile for your readers. You can help make their experience more memorable by personally signing your book and perhaps providing a quick note. You'll be surprised. You don't have to be a world-famous author for readers to be thrilled that they received an autographed book. The important thing is that the book is now special as it's been personalized by the author. I mean, how many people do you know off the top of your head with an autographed book?

Before you race off to sign your first book, there are a couple of tips that you should consider. You might want to think about where the best spot to autograph your book is. It's commonly done on the title page, but the author gets the last say. Perhaps you think your signature will look better on the inside cover of the book. It's a personal preference, I suppose.

Personalize the message to the person you're signing the book for; use their name or give some type of cue in the message so that years later they'll remember the significance of the note. Lastly, don't forget to include a signature phrase and then your autograph. Examples of such phrases are "thanks," "warm wishes," and "best regards." It's a good idea to have a queue of signature phrases in place so that you can rotate them with each book you sign. Here are more suggestions when it comes to signing your book:

- **Practice your signature:** You don't want to scribble some gibberish onto your dedicated fan's book. Show that you care and practice your signature so that it's a fine work of art. Well, maybe that's a bit too much, but I'm sure you get the point ;). An example of a pretty swell signature is that of Walt Disney.[14]

- **Protect yourself:** It's not a bad idea to make your signature different than your legal name. Hey, maybe one day soon you'll become famous and you don't want to be the target of identity theft.

- **Use a good pen:** A permanent pen with archival ink is an unbeatable combination. You don't want the ink to smear years down the road. A popular brand for these types of pens is *Sharpie*.

- **Consider bookplates:** These are labels you can attach to books to indicate who the owner is. They can be purchased on Amazon in packs at an affordable rate.

- **Add dates:** When you date the signature and message, it helps to personalize it. It's like how dates help personalize letters sent via snail mail.

Ship internationally: By making giveaways available to contestants in more countries, you increase your exposure. If you're shipping a physical version of your book, then this could be expensive. However, let's think about it in another way. If a book costs you $40 to ship, but generates 20 sales at $7.95 royalty as a result of the exposure from the contest, then wouldn't that investment be worth it? You bet it would.

According to Alexa.com, the United States consists of the largest demographic of users of Goodreads so there's a high probability that the winner of the contest would be located in the U.S. However, if you get a winner that's located internationally, then be prepared to live up to your promise and ship to them. As mentioned previously, you may have to eat a fat shipping fee, but by increasing the numbers of locations you ship to, you not only give avid readers internationally a chance to read your book, but you most likely generate more publicity as well.

Amp up your marketing: Even though Goodreads have millions of registered book readers, there's no guarantee your giveaway will gain traction. Now it's time to step up the marketing. Remember, your book is like your baby so no one should be more proactive in promoting it than you. Here are some ideas to get the juices flowing.

If you own any social media properties, then make sure to share your contest with followers. This is something that will hopefully get your fans rallied up and spreading the word about your book promo. Also, you should be doing the little things to help build up your credibility on the Goodreads website. The easiest way to do this is to get acquainted with all the core features of the site and become an engaged user. If you can make the website fun, then the marketing will come naturally. It will feel more like a game than a chore.

Some ways to become "engaged" are to join discussions, participate in groups,[15] add friends,[16] purchase ads,[17] add an event,[18] review books you read,[19] and participate in the Ask the Author program.[20] Also, continual learning and testing is a surefire strategy for growing your followers on Goodreads. The more followers you have, the more you increase your presence within Goodreads.

LinkedIn

LinkedIn is one of my favorite social media sites. I find that the time I invest in it is mostly connected to my professional life. It's also a highly-overlooked source for discovering reviewers for your book. One of the powerful features of LinkedIn is the ability to rekindle and expand your professional networks.

To get started, create an account,[21] add connections you know from your professional/personal life,[22] and seek professionals who fall under the umbrella of your targeted book readers. When you send them a connection request, make sure to personalize the message and tell them the reason you believe it makes sense for the two of you to connect. Make sure to engage in the LinkedIn ecosystem by posting content, liking content,[23] adding comments,[24] joining/participating in groups,[25] and sharing content with your network that you find useful.[26] Once you have established an audience, you can create a post offering a digital or physical giveaway of your book. You build good karma in the ecosystem as you're providing connections with something of utmost value. The more buzz you generate about your giveaway, the more publicity your book gets.

When you use this approach, you're using the *pull vs. push* tactic in marketing. With this technique, reviewers are approaching you, which means that there's a high chance they're interested in reading what you have. For example, say you create a post on LinkedIn in which you're giving away 20 digital copies of your book. If you have 5,000 connections that are target readers for the content of your book, then there's a high probability your giveaway will generate tremendous publicity on the network.

Twitter

This is the famous microblogging network utilized by authors to increase their platform. My advice is to make use of the search option to scout for the right reviewers. The funny thing is you don't need a large following or even an account to get started with the research process. There are some Twitter users who are huge book fanatics and they review a wide variety of them. I prefer to not contact these individuals as they'll most likely already have a large workload. Instead, I would rather target Twitter users who will have a high interest in the content of my book.

In order to target these users, we need to narrow the search results in Twitter and then discover the best way to reach them. One way to do this is to filter results by using the Twitter search engine.[27] Like Google, Twitter provides advanced filtering techniques for narrowing down results. There's quite a list of advance operators in Twitter. Trying to memorize all of them if you're not an active user is probably a moot point. To use advance search in Twitter, visit the Advance Search form.[28]

The advance search feature that I found myself using frequently is the "none of these words" option. It helps exclude results I'm not interested in and helps me find the profiles of my targeted reader much quicker. For example, if I was looking for "java book reviews," I may get several extraneous results. The reason for this is because "java" can be associated with either coffee or the computer programming language. Since I'm seeking for results dealing with the latter, I may want to exclude the keyword "coffee" from the results.

Once you have compiled a list of Twitter users who show strong interest in the type of book you have, the next step is to find a way to reach out to them. Now, this can be a little tricky because at the time of this publication, users can only *direct message* those who are following them, or those who have modified their settings so that anyone can send them a direct message.

However, if neither of these options apply to the user you're trying to reach, then you have to be more creative in your approach. One, if the person lists their website on their profile, then you're in luck! You can visit their website and look for a contact page. If they don't have a website, but if the person is using their real name, then you can try searching for them in Google to see if they have any additional social media presences like Facebook or LinkedIn. If they do, then great; send them a connection request explaining why you would like to connect. If they accept, contact them with the proposition you have.

If you can't find their information on outside social media sites, then you could consider mentioning them in a tweet which appears in the recipient's notifications tab.[29] To do this, compose a tweet and tag them in the message using the ampersand (@) symbol.

Reddit

A long-long-time-ago Digg was the undisputed heavyweight champion of the social news world. Fast forward to the present and Digg has been dethroned and replaced with a new king in the social media realm: Reddit. This is a social news site in which users can engage with others of similar interests around content. I would argue that the true magic of Reddit doesn't happen on the homepage, but in the subreddits, or topic specific categories of the site. Users can create an account and engage in the network by liking, commenting, sharing, or creating content. After you create an account, the next step is to gather active subreddits and get involved. Reddit is a virtual community and, like a traditional community, if you disrupt the tranquility of it then you will be expelled from it.

An attractive feature of Reddit is that users can self-govern the site through their use of voting. If users like content then they *upvote* it and if they dislike content then they effectively *downvote* it. You can learn about the basics of Reddit by reading their FAQs.[30] It's also a good idea to get familiar with reddiquette.[31]

The first step is creating your account.[32] Once that's done, think of a simple executable strategy. You may decide to subscribe to active subreddits related to your niche, read community guidelines, selflessly contribute, and then if all the previous goes well, then ask for permission to host a giveaway. You need to receive the graces of the moderators of the subreddit.

Now, let's walk through a hypothetical situation on how to execute such a marketing campaign. Let's assume that I wrote a book about classic cars and that I wanted to host a giveaway by providing free copies of the digital version of my book to related subreddits. Let's get to it.

There are two methods that I use to discover new subreddits. One, I can use Reddit's internal search engine,[33] which you can utilize once you sign up for the site, or two, I use an external search engine like Google. This explanation will be done with Google. Enter the following query to discover subreddits related to the genre of your book: *keywords* site:www.reddit.com

Building upon the example, the search query to find subreddits related to classic cars would look like the following:

classic cars site:www.reddit.com

After pruning through the search results, I discovered two subreddits called classic cars[34] and muscle cars.[35] The bigger subreddit is classic cars, and at the time of publication, it had 30,429 subscribers with at least 100 users online during any point of time. These numbers aren't outstanding, but the good thing is this subreddit is concentrated mainly on folks who are not just interested in classic cars, but are passionate about it, which would make it worth my while to engage in this community.

In addition to opportunities to promote your book giveaway, subreddits provide additional benefits, such as a place to establish credibility, do market research, and network with website owners in your niche. Also, you can discover different but similar subreddits by analyzing the right-hand column of the subreddit. Lots of recommended subreddits is a good problem to have. It's a problem because it increases your workload, but it's beneficial as you can significantly increase the promotional opportunities for your book. It makes sense to start with the largest and most active subreddits.

Once you discovered it, subscribe to it and start becoming an engaged member. Doing so should be easy. After all, you wrote a book related to the topic! Vote on content, add comments, submit new content, and constantly seek out ways in which you can enrich the community.

Once you have built up karma (which you can obtain from submitting useful links and posting helpful comments) you can contact the moderators offering to host a free book giveaway. Remember, any website that has many active users will be targeted by spammers and Reddit is no different. They have grown accustomed to people joining and trying to leech off the network. However, this type of "marketing" is superficial and shortsighted. A better approach is to think for the long haul. Add value first and then ask to host a giveaway. This would provide the community even more value. Doing so will more than likely increase your chances of moderators approving your proposition, but it will also increase your chances of them supporting you if you have worked hard to add tremendous value to the community.

CHAPTER VII:
Event Hosting

Hosting an event is an excellent way for authors to gain publicity, make sales, and build their fan base. A popular example of an author-related event is a book signing in which the author arrives at a venue, interact with attendees, and sells their books.

When I first got started, I had no idea about all of the intricacies involved with hosting an author event. Lots of calls had to be made, appearances on local radio were required, and ads had to be run. However, before you set off making phone calls to arrange your first book signing event, I want to provide you with as many tips and anecdotes as possible so that your first signing event will be a success.

I had to learn how to properly conduct a book signing event the hard way. It was conducted at a little independent bookstore in a small city in western Arizona. I didn't discover it by searching for it online; I actually found it serendipitously while on vacation and exploring the downtown area. The owner was polite, and gave me the opportunity to host a book signing. I was thrilled! However, I was brought back down to reality when the book signing occurred. The results were embarrassing to say the least. The planning was poor on my end and I didn't do nearly enough promotion for the event. Even worse, I made my decision based on emotion as opposed to logic.

On the day of the book signing, the customers that came in were mostly purchasing books about fantasy. I like reading that genre, but it wasn't what the topic of my book was about. Many lessons were learned that day and they will be elaborated on throughout this chapter.

Even though book signing events can be a lot of work, when well-planned and executed, they can also be loads of fun. All that hard gets paid off when you have interesting discussions about your book with readers and begin racking in sales.

Bookstores

Even though they're slowly dwindling in popularity, bookstores are still a good source to host your book-related event. After all, it's probably a decent probability that book lovers would congregate here. There's Barnes & Noble and then there're smaller, independent shops. All of the options will be exhausted along with tips on how to go about arranging your book-related event.

Barnes & Noble: This is the king of retail bookstores. It has over 770 bookstores in all 50 states in the U.S. Therefore, regardless of the genre of your book, Barnes & Noble will most likely have readers interested in it. However, getting your event hosted with Barnes & Noble can be a challenge for first time self-publishers. There are a couple of things that you need to know.

Barnes & Noble will typically require that your book is stored in their warehouse. That way, when it's time for your book signing, they can easily order copies of it for your event. You can learn about the steps you'll need to take in order to get your books into their retail stores by reading the article, "Consideration for Product Listing on BN.com and Retail Store Placement."[1] The review process typically takes three months.

You might have better luck going to smaller, independent bookstores as they have the authority to make direct decisions like this. However, with Barnes & Noble, their decision process is mandated to their headquarters in NYC. You do, however, have the capability to sell your book on their website: BN.com. You can do this with CreateSpace by choosing expanded distribution. What happens is that your book will become available via Lightning Source–they have the capability to make CreateSpace titles, along with other POD titles, available through BN.com.[2] This is not the same as having your title available on the shelves of a retail store. If your book does get approved to be placed in their retail stores, then scheduling a book signing event simply comes down to contacting the store manager at the location you're interested in.

Powell's Books: If you have ever been to Portland, Oregon and love books, then chances are you might have visited Powell Books (PB).[3] What makes PB unique is that they're the largest independent bookstore chain in the United States. All of their stores are located in the beautiful state of Oregon. In order to host a book signing event at Powell's, you'll need to first get your book in their stores. After that's done, the next step to the equation is to contact the event manager and negotiate the event details. To learn how to submit your book for consideration in Powell's, you should read the article on their site titled: "Small Press Publishers. Interested in Listing Your Books with Powell's Books."[4]

Local indie bookstores: If you can't host a book signing at Barnes & Noble or Powell's, then you should consider the smaller but cozier independent bookstores. The key for this is to start locally and then expand outwards. To discover independent bookstores in your area, just run this query into a search engine: *independent bookstores state*

For example, if you want to see independent bookstores in *California*, you will run this query into a search engine: *independent bookstores California*

Next, analyze the results carefully and select the bookstores you feel will be a good fit. This is the tricky part, so here are some tips. I would recommend visiting their website or social media pages. If you see that the bookstore advertises certain genre books on their homepage, then that may be a good indicator of what their customers like. You should also pay close attention to their social media profiles like Facebook. If you see that the bookstore commonly hosts author events related to children's books, then this is a good hint that this is the hot commodity of the store. If you want a sure-fire idea of what some of their bestselling books are, you can simply pick up the phone and ask to speak to a store manager or someone else who would be able to provide you these details. You can alternatively send them an email.

Let's look at an example to get a better idea of how to go about looking for bookstores to host your author-related event. Let's say that you wrote a book about *computer programming*. When you search for independent bookstores, you may find stores that specialize in literature and arts. Since this genre has little to do with computer programming, I would recommend moving along. After narrowing my results, I started to look for independent stores that emphasized technical books. After digging around, I discovered universities have bookstores on campus, making them prime candidates to host book signing events. There are over two thousand universities in the United States alone! These are excellent venues to host events at.

Libraries

These educational hubs go back centuries and are excellent resources for authors to not only get research done, but to present their book to a community of avid readers. Regardless of where you live, you're bound to find a library nearby.

Here's my advice. Go to local libraries and establish cordial relationships with the librarians. The good thing about libraries is that they host a myriad of genres. Therefore, it doesn't matter if you're working on the next American classic or if you're writing a book about international politics, a well-stocked library should cater to the interests of an array of readers. Here are some tips on how self-published authors can host their book signing event at libraries.

Start local: Here's a fun fact. There are over 100,000 libraries in the United States! This means that there are tons (literally) of libraries that you can tap into. However, let's keep things simple in the beginning. My advice is to start locally and then scale outward. You'll conserve money for transportation and lodging by remaining local. To find libraries near you, type in this query into a search engine: *libraries near me*

This will provide you a list of libraries along with important information like the URL, address, and phone numbers. I would recommend compiling a list in a spreadsheet program like Google Sheets[5] to keep this information organized.

Be fully prepared: Make sure you have all the basics covered. You should go in with the same exact concept of pitching books to bookstores. Libraries have budgets like any other institution, and they want books that their members will borrow. If the library has a calendar of events, then that's a good source for inspiration.

Go to their sites: Most libraries will have a contact page on their site so that you can submit your inquiry and wait for a response. You can always follow up with the library by phone if you haven't heard back from them in two weeks. Libraries are busy, especially the bigger ones, so patience is important when trying to work something out. Also, it's a good idea to know the types of events the library is used to hosting. Again, this information should be listed somewhere on the library's site, typically under an events or calendar page. You may need to do some maneuvering on the site as most libraries' websites are slightly different. It's also helpful to understand how the library system in your area works. It's common for there to be a main branch library in an area, which makes decisions for their smaller regional libraries. For example, the Burton Barr Central Library[6] is the central library in the Phoenix area. It makes the decisions for its smaller branches, so if you want to get your book in the Yucca Library in Phoenix, then it has to go through the administration of the Burton Barr library.

Meetup

Meetup is a social-networking site that's based around the concept of people meeting other like-minded folks for some type of event. It can be used to make new friends, have discussions about various topics, or to learn a new hobby. There are many Meetups located across various parts of the world. If a group of people are interested in a certain thing, and if your book contains information about it, then wouldn't it make sense to host a book signing event with the group? I'd say so. Therefore, let's discover the basics about Meetup. com through the use of a concrete example.

Let's assume that "Mary" is a linguist and she wrote a book that teaches how to speak Spanish. She lives in San Francisco and is willing to travel 25 miles outside the city. What are her options? Well, the first step she should take is to visit the homepage of Meetup.[7] This website uses geo-targeting so it delivers content to visitors based on their location. This makes sense because it wouldn't be helpful for a user in Paris, France to be served Meetups from NYC. When Mary visits Meetup.com, she'll be served the events that are available to people within 25 miles of San Francisco[8] by default.

From there she can scan various groups to discover which one would make sense for her to form a partnership with. After spending several minutes digging through the results, she discovers that a couple of groups fit the criterions, which are:

- San Francisco Spanish Language Meetup

- SF Babel: International Exchange
- SpanFran: French/Spanish/English Exchange

The next steps Sarah can take are to attend one of the Meetups in person, mingle with the group members, and get in contact with the host to pitch her proposal.

If the Meetup is large then it's not uncommon for it to have multiple organizers, so knowing the right person to contact can be a little tricky. What should Mary do? Well, she can look at the list of organizers by clicking on the Organizers link which appears under the gray text, "Members." From there she can look for the boss which will have the title, *Organizer*. The organizer in a Meetup can point others to help manage their group, but none of them can have the title of organizer. Instead, they will be given the titles of co-organizer, assistant organizer, or event organizer.[9]

Once Mary gets in contact with the right person, she can pitch them her idea. If all goes well, Mary could consider looking for similar Meetups in other cities. The more public appearances Mary makes, the more confidence she gains and will learn from past experience on how she can better conduct a book signing event.

Museums

The first thing that probably comes to mind when you think of museums are artistic masterpieces from talented artists. While this is true, I want you to know that there are museums dedicated to everything under the sun. There are museums for human hair,[10] bad art,[11] and ramen noodles.[12] Well, if there are museums dedicated to these topics, then I'm sure that you could find museums dedicated to the topic of your book, right? The first step is to use a search engine to filter results for museums that would most closely match the genre of your book. For example, let's say that Mike is a first-time author from Iowa who wrote a book about motorcycle maintenance. He doesn't know off the top of his mind if there are motorcycle museums out there, so he turns to his favorite search engine and enters this query: *motorcycle museum in iowa*

To his surprise, he discovers that there's a motorcycle museum in Anamosa,

Iowa which is 50 minutes from where he's at. As a matter of fact, the museum constantly hosts events. This seems like a good opportunity so he contacts the event manager to make a pitch. This process could be repeated with similar museums to increase the number of appearances an author makes.

Eventbrite

According to their website, Eventbrite[13] is the world's largest event technology platform. If you want to plan, finance, and host your very own event from scratch, then this is the platform I'd recommend. Even if you're hosting your event at a public institution such as a library, Eventbrite can help you manage your event along with aiding in keeping track of analytics.

Even if you have no interest in hosting your own event, this is still a helpful site for discovering events based on interests. You may discover a new musical festival happening next week, hooplas for the upcoming holiday, or an industry-related conference. So whether you want to host your own event or discover more networking opportunities, this is a good site to check out.

Since this book is dedicated to self-published authors who want to get ahead and build their fan base, I'll cover the basics of how you can use Eventbrite to host your book-related event.

To learn the basics about Eventbrite, read the Eventbrite Help Center.[14] Let's gain a feel for how Eventbrite works by using a concrete example. Let's say that Denzel is a NYC-based author that wants to host a book signing for his cookbook. He has spent the past six months working hard on his social media game and has built a combined social media following of 45,000 across various channels like Facebook, Twitter, and Instagram.

He's confident that due to the engagement of his followers and various surveys that he can fill out a room of 50 attendees. He strategically targeted social media users in NYC and already has ideas on where he can host his book signing. However, he has never done a book signing before so he wants to research book signings in NYC so that he can generate more ideas. He plans to attend one or two so that he can see firsthand how to run one.

The first step he takes is visiting Eventbrite's homepage.[13] Like Meetup, Eventbrite will show you events based on your IP location. You can easily change the events shown by entering the keyword of the city you wish to explore in the "city or location" field.

After looking through the results, Denzel grew frustrated as there were too many results not in alignment with what he's interested in. He sees events for real estate, parties, and popup dinners, but nothing related to book signings. So, he goes back to the Eventbrite homepage and filters his results by adding in the keywords "book signing." When the results were generated, he's happy to notice that he now has over 400 book signing events to analyze.

On the first page results, he sees a chef in NYC that will be holding a book signing soon. Curious, he clicks on the event to discover more. The creative juices are flowing for Denzel and he continues searching through the results to see if he can gain more inspiration from authors who are hosting book signing events in the area.

He checks out another author who wrote a book about acting and discovers that even though their book is in a completely different genre, he still got some inspiration by reading their event description. After digging around on various author events in NYC and taking notes, Denzel is excited and decides that it was time for him to start planning his own event on Eventbrite.

He makes a few calls to some local businesses to reserve a spot for his venue. Now that he has a location, his next step is to develop a strategy for promoting his event. After digging around on the web, he learns that as long you're hosting a free event, Eventbrite won't charge you anything. You can learn more about creating events by reading the "How to create an event"[15] article. Denzel does have plans to host paid events in the future, so he reads an article about the different packages Eventbrite offers along with the payouts (when hosts get paid).[16]

There are three main packages with Eventbrite: essentials, professional, and premium. Both essentials and professional cost nothing to use for free events. However, if you're selling tickets, then the costing structure varies by sale. For example, the *essentials* cost 1% + $0.99 per paid ticket, and professional costs 2.5% + $1.99 per paid ticket.

If you're selling a ticket that's priced at $14.95, here are the expenses the transaction will have based on the package you choose and the ticket price of $14.95:

Essentials: $14.95 - ($14.95 * .01 + .99) = $13.8. Costs $1.1 per transaction
Professional: $14.95 - ($14.95 * .025 +1.99) = $12.6. Costs 2.4 per transaction

The difference between these two packages comes down to the number of features. The essentials package, as the name indicates, provides the bare essentials you need to get up and running. With this package, you can provide only one ticket type, have all of the ticketing/registration essentials, and have your event listed on Eventbrite and partner's websites.[17] The professional package comes with everything that the essential package does, but with extra perks such as unlimited ticket types, the option to sell tickets on your own site, customizable checkout forms, detailed sales analytics, and reserved seating.[18] The premium package is tailored to organizations with large and complex events, so if you're hosting your first book signing, then this probably won't apply to you.

Selecting which option is best for you boils down to the number of features you realistically expect to use. If you're unsure of which package to use, then you can always start with essential and then upgrade to professional if needed in the future. You can learn how to change your Eventbrite package[19] by reading their help center.

It's important to note that Eventbrite has an in-house payment processor called Eventbrite Payment Processing (EPP).[20] If you use EPP, then you have the option to pass the fees along to the customer so you won't pay anything out of pocket—you can also use the money that you receive from the event sales to pay for the fees.

If you use a third-party processor like PayPal or Authorize.net, then you'll receive an invoice for the fees. Eventbrite wants users to use their in-house processor which is the default payment option—if hosts use a different processor, then certain features like registration transfers are disabled. To read the features that are disabled with the use of a third party payment processor, read the article: "What features are unavailable with PayPal and Authorize.net?"[21] Note: hosts can also accept offline payments like checks and money orders by setting up offline payments.[22] When an attendee registers for an event through Eventbrite Payment Processing, they stay on the site to complete their purchase and are charged 3% per transaction. This fee is automatically collected. Direct deposits[23] are the quickest way to get paid with Eventbrite and payments are released 4-5 days after the event.

Let's transition back to the example. Denzel easily figures out how to get the event up and running. He knows that was the simple part. Now comes the hard part which is increasing event awareness. The phrase "if you build it, they will come" is true to an extent. If you build something remarkable, that's great, but you still need to let people know about it so that they can spread the word. Following are several methods you can use to increase the publicity of your Eventbrite listing.

Eventbrite SEO: When you create an event on Eventbrite, an SEO-friendly URL will automatically be generated. This is the URL you can share with others so they can see your event details and register for it. However, the URL is not the only SEO principle you should be concerned about. You should ensure that the title and description for your event include the appropriate keywords that prospective attendees would enter into Eventbrite's search engine. The settings for events by default is public meaning that it's accessible everywhere, including the search engines–this is an option that you would want to leave alone to increase your visibility. Eventbrite also gives hosts the opportunity to categorize their events so it's important you take advantage of this feature.

Attractive & detailed event page: The events page is where you'll make or break your chances for promoting your event. There are two variables that you need to concentrate on. One, you need to get people to the events page. Two, you need to get them to register. You may want to consider giving the event a distinct and catchy name. Just think about some of the most popular events globally: Mardi Gras, Oktoberfest, Coachella, Glastonbury, Burning Man, and the Super Bowl. These all have memorable names, which is a nice complement for social media as they can be easily converted into hash tags for additional promotion. It's also very important to put the exact location of the event on Google Maps along with driving instructions from several nearby points-of-interest just in case an attendee's GPS fails them. I personally use Eventbrite to discover interesting venues when traveling. It really annoys me when the host is meager on details. This should not be the case. Instead, provide as much details about your event as possible.

After all, in a busy-modern-society, having people show up for your event is kind of a big deal. Helpful details such as parking information, faqs, age requirements, and refund policy will not only help inform your attendees, but assist with search engine visibility as you're adding more content to your event page.

The content on your event page doesn't all have to be textual. There's various media that you can add to your event listing in order to make it more compelling. Things like images and videos are worth considering to give your listing more character. If you plan to make an event a recurring one, whether yearly, monthly, or weekly, then you can consider having a logo created for it. If the event is an extension of your company, you could also consider using your company logo. If you don't want to use any logos, then what you could do is use a stock photo to help set the mood for your event.

For example, if you're hosting a fancy-schmancy cheese-and-wine event, then a stock photo of a gala makes sense, or if you plan on hosting a music festival, then an image of a music concert fits the bill. Just like how your social media pages are extensions of your brand, your Eventbrite listing should be no different. It's not a bad idea to customize your event page with a unique header and footer.[24]

Email invitations: Once your event is live, Eventbrite allows you to send email notifications of up to 2,000 guests per day.[25] This can be an excellent opportunity to get the ball rolling for your first event, but treading cautiously is recommended. One, it's well known that spam is not tolerated, and that there are laws in place to combat it.[26] Two, if your emails have a high percentage of bounces, unsubscribes, or undeliverables, then there's a good chance Eventbrite will limit the number of invites you send. Therefore, to be on the safe side, you should avoid unsolicited invites.[27]

Sync attendees: If you create a popular event, that's fine and dandy, but what happens once your event ends? Well, if you have other products, promotions, or events, you can stay in contact with those who attended by synching them with email software. Building and maintaining an active email list is crucial for businesses that rely heavily on web promotion. It's a low cost, high return marketing method. Eventbrite has a repository of extensions, known as the Eventbrite Spectrum[28] that increase the flexibility of the web app. If you're using a popular email software, then there's a good chance it's available in the repository.

Affiliate program: Eventbrite enables hosts with the power to manage their own affiliate program, which provides a commission for those who promote your event. The promoter gets a special link, known as an affiliate link, which tracks the number of referrals they send through it. You can send invites to personal contacts, make it public by posting the signup link on the event page, or send emails to the attendees, letting them know that you have an affiliate program. To learn more about how affiliate programs operate, you can read the "How to increase ticket sales with an affiliate pro- gram"[29] article in the Eventbrite help center.

Purchase advertising: Eventbrite is a popular website in itself. With millions of active users, there are ample opportunities you can take advantage of to increase the popularity of your events within its ecosystem. With promoted listings, you can target attendees by various parameters, such as city, category, or keywords. Doing so maximizes the chance of your event being seen by the most people possible.

This is a form of native advertising and you pay whenever impressions are served. It's different from pay-per-click advertising like AdWords, which charges by the click. With promoted listings, you have the ability to start, stop, or extend your promotion any time.

In order to track your campaign's activity you'll need to install the promoted listings extension.[30] At the time of publication, promoted listings are charged $40 for every 1,000 impressions. So, if your budget is $100, then you can expect to generate 2,500 impressions. Read Eventbrite's Help Center to learn how to setup promoted listings[31] and manage/optimize them.[32] Promoted listings are only available in 10 cities at the time of publication, which are:

- Atlanta
- Boston
- Chicago
- London
- Los Angeles
- Miami
- New York City
- Philadelphia
- San Francisco
- Washington DC

If promoted listings are not available in the city your event will occur, then you can consider placing your event in an Eventbrite attendee newsletter.[33] This is available in many more cities in the U.S., U.K., and Ireland. These are algorithmically-generated emails sent to various cities every Thursday.

The price will be based on the size of the city and the average open rate. At the time of publication, the cheapest email option is $100 and the most expensive one is $600. If you're interested in having your event advertised via email, then you can fill out the Eventbrite's Attendee Email form.[34]

Discount codes: You can provide discounts to your event as an incentive to increase the velocity at which your attendees register. For the complete steps on how to enable and configure discounts for your events, read the article, "How to set up discount codes for one or multiple events."[35] There is also something known as *access tickets* which you can set up for a select group of people like sponsors or members of the press/media. In order for the discount to be processed, the person must enter the correct password. To learn how to create these, read the article, "How to set up access codes for hidden tickets for one or multiple events."[36]

Add your event to Facebook: If you have ever registered for an event on Facebook, then more than likely you saw an Eventbrite-based event embedded into the fan page. Eventbrite makes it easy for hosts to add their listing to their fan page. You need to use the *Add to Facebook* tool, which you can learn more about on the "How to add your Eventbrite event to Face- book and sell tickets" page.[37] This can only be done on a public Facebook fan page, so you can't add an event to a personal account or a group.

Promoting Events Locally

There are a plethora of resources that event hosts can tap into in order to generate local interest to their event. Just like how cities have varying media outlets that cater to the interests of their demographics, cities also have local sites that provide news and current events happening in the surrounding area. It's important to locate these sites and use them as leverage for your event promotion. Implement the following strategies and you'll be on your way to increasing the awareness of your event.

Gather your details: The sooner the better. All of the popular events you hear about are pre-marketed well in advance as it gives the event host proper time to promote the event. It also allows attendees enough time to make travel arrangements such as modes of transportation and accommodation, if needed. Everyone is busy these days so planning an event last minute is not recommended. Also, some local sites won't accept submission to events that are being held on a short notice. Therefore, make sure you have all of the details for your event. Venue, dates, and time should be figured out well in advance from the event date.

Enter the right queries: If you want to discover websites in which you can submit your local event to, then enter the query: *submit event + city name.* For example, to discover websites you can submit an event to in Houston, the query will be *submit event houston,* and for the city of Philadelphia, it would be *submit event philadelphia.* Typing in a query like *phoenix events* is too broad. It may very well give you sites that allow you to submit events, but you'll have to filter the results extensively to find what you want. Also, a good portion of those sites won't allow users to submit events. Therefore, to save yourself time during the searching process, it's a good idea to craft a more specific search query.

Read guidelines then submit: Most local event directories will have submission guidelines for eligible submissions. For example, one media site I researched only allows nonprofit organizations to submit events while another one didn't allow nonprofit organizations at all! Others only allowed events happening at least four weeks from now, while others had more lenient policies. The submission guidelines should all be listed on the page in which you fill out your event details.

Once you find local event directories you can submit to, create a unique Eventbrite URL to track the results of each site. You can use a URL-management service such as Bitly[38] or Google URL Shortener.[39] I would recommend a spreadsheet program so you can separate the data easily. I prefer to use Google Spreadsheets.[40] This will help you keep track of the number of clicks you received from each site, enabling you to evolve your marketing strategies.

Become Your Own Publicist

One of my biggest regrets when publishing my first book is that I didn't create an author media kit. I didn't really have a decent understanding of it and since I didn't see many authors do it, I didn't believe that it was that crucial for promoting my book. However, fast-forward to the present and I can't believe how wrong I was about this. A media kit is not only helpful for members of the press, but it also makes life a lot easier when you want to pitch your book to indie shops, local retailers, libraries, college bookstores, or anywhere else where selling your book could be a possibility. If you were to check out some of the authors on the New York Times best-selling list, then there's a high probability the bulk of them have a media kit on their website. It's important, and creating a nice media kit can help push the sales of your books or even speaking engagements. There's no standardization on what must be included in a media kit. However, by analyzing the owners of several best-selling books I saw some recurring patterns on what authors typically include in their media kit.

Author bio: You wrote a book! There's no time for you to be timid or shy about it. As a matter of fact, unless you hired a publicist, there's a good chance that not many people will volunteer to talk about your book, so you need to be the driving force behind it. Writing a book has similarities to starting a grassroots program. You're the fuel, the spark, the catalyst for taking the book and pushing it to the attention of the masses.

Before you start working on your bio, step back and think about some of your favorite people in this world. It can be someone you personally know, or it can be a person you admire from the distance like a celebrity. Think about their story and how you recall it. You're most likely familiar with their origins and may even know some of their biggest achievements in life.

Now, it's time to focus in on yourself. You want to make your bio enthralling to read while shedding light on why you're qualified to write the book in the first place. Some topics you may want to discuss are education, career milestones, personal experience, and stories that you wish to share with the world. Your story should be so exciting, so interesting, that it's good enough to be shown on TV.

If you're struggling developing your bio, then consider reaching out to someone who knows you personally and ask them to write a recommendation for you. A trusted colleague could be a good place to start. It can be difficult... maybe even uncomfortable writing about ourselves so getting an outside perspective could help stimulate the creative juices.

Here's an alternative perspective. Imagine that someone was interested in writing a memoir about your professional life–think carefully about the things you want included in it. Some of these professional experiences could be expanded on to be included in your bio. One of the tricky things that stump writers is what *grammatical person* it should be written in. There are many different schools of thoughts with this. Some writers believe that writing in first person is conceited while others think that writing in third person is pretentious. To be technical about it, if you're writing your bio yourself then it should be in first person, and if someone else writes your bio, then it should be in third person.

Book details: If you want to sell more copies of your books, then it helps to make the book buyer's life easier. One way to do this is to list all the book details a prospective buyer needs in order to make an informed purchasing decision. Some of these details are listed below:

- Author
- Publisher
- Word count
- ISBN (digital)
- ISBN (print)
- Book description
- Where to purchase (Amazon, Barnes & Noble, Powell)
- Distributors
- Wholesalers
- Publication date
- Price
- Dimensions

These details will be asked on a recurring basis, so having all of the important details consolidated into one easy-to-find location will help you be prepared.

Media

Authors should create content that can be used by members of the press, like reporters or journalists. This can help increase the publicity of the book and push sales. Below is a list of media content authors can make available to the press:

Headshots: Having a professional headshot can do wonders for public relations. It helps to have pictures in high-resolution, various colors, and multiple image formats. As the name indicates, a headshot should emphasize the face, so there shouldn't be any objects in the photo that distracts from this. Depending on the author's style, they can opt in for a more casual picture that gives the viewer more insights into their personality. For example, a naturalist who self-published a book may opt to have their photo taken in a national park. Hiring someone who takes photos for a living is probably your best bet to have the highest quality picture possible.

Book artwork: Having your book artwork available makes it easy for others to share it. For example, let's say that a popular blogger in your niche requests a copy of your book so that they can review it. After reading it, they like it a lot and want to publish a review on their site. However, there's one issue, they want to add the book cover image to their blog but can't find it. What you can do is attach an image of your book or link to the URL on your site. Having various sizes of your book cover is never a negative, so the bloggers will most likely not have an issue with adding it to their site. Also, from my experience, including a book cover image helps to garner interest in it when requesting reviews.

Articles: Do you have articles that generate some buzz on the web? Including some of your best pieces of writing can provide the media a peek into your writing style and establish credibility. If they like the way you write and the ideas you share then this can help persuade them to reach out to you for public appearances.

Audio: Have you ever been interviewed before? It could be offline on a local radio or online on a podcast. If so, you can include links to the audio files to provide the media with a glimpse of your personality. Being charismatic definitely helps you to gain more media appearances. Just take a look at some of the most popular TV hosts like Stephen Colbert or Oprah Winfrey. They're "made for TV" as they have an engaging personality that attracts millions of viewers to tune into them. I'm not saying that you have to be as seasoned as a TV host, but being able to give interesting interviews is never a bad skill for authors to have under their belt.

Videos: Have you given a lecture, talk, or workshop and have any video recording of it? Including links to your videos helps viewers see your presentation skills and could increase your speaking gigs.

Free-parts: If you self-published a book then you have full control over your work. Therefore, if you want to provide free excerpts from your book such as table of contents, intro, or a free chapter, then you're more than welcome to do so. This can help prospective readers see snippets of your content and entice them to purchase.

Reviews: Have you received positive endorsements about your book? Including these in your media kit can help foster credibility and increase sales. Make sure to include all appropriate details about the reviewer in their review.

Excerpts: Do you have any favorite parts from your book? If so, include it in your media kit. Just think of excerpts like the short clips that they show for upcoming movies to tease the audience. By providing your most interesting content to the media, it can help build interest for your book.

Interview questions: Are you interested in being interviewed on a local radio show or podcast? Well, you can make the host's job easier by providing them with a list of questions they can choose from. This can help them facilitate the conversation during the interview, and by listing the questions, you can help prep yourself for the discussion. The answers shouldn't be scripted as doing so may make the conversation seem mechanical. However, there's nothing wrong with coming prepared and having a good idea of what the conversation will be about.

Contact information: Providing a variety of ways in which the media can get in contact with you is essential if you want more opportunities. Common contact methods that authors provide are phone and email. If you prefer to not disclose your personal phone number, then you can use a service like Google Voice.[41] In addition, you can provide other avenues for media to get in contact with you such as social media accounts like Facebook, Twitter, and LinkedIn, or even through apps like Skype.[42]

Formatting: Once you assembled all the information for the media kit, it's important you go over it so that you have the best presentation possible. At the bare minimum, re-read through your information to ensure that everything is correct and that there are no grammatical or typographical errors.

Once that's done you may want to consider adding headings and sub-headings so that members of the media can easily locate the details they're looking for. If the media kit is a huge chunk of text with little spacing, then finding certain things will be a challenge. Also, you may want to consider making multiple formats for your media kit. You can of course pull up a word processor, add all the details, and then wrap all that data in a pdf file. However, something you could also consider is parsing the data from the different sections of your media kit and using it for content on your author website. For example, the content that you create for your bio could easily be content for the about page, and the details for getting in touch with you can go on the contact page.

Resources

Chapter I Resources

Amazon:

[1]Amazon Best Sellers:
https://www.amazon.com/best-sellers-books-Amazon/zgbs/books

[2] Arts & Photography Best Sellers:
https://www.amazon.com/Best-Sellers-Books-Arts-Photography/zgbs/books/1/ref=zg_bs_nav_b_1_b

[3] Business & Money:
https://www.amazon.com/Best-Sellers-Books-Business-Money/zgbs/books/3/ref=zg_bs_nav_b_1_b

[4] Humor & Entertainment:
https://www.amazon.com/Best-Sellers-Books-Humor-Entertainment/zgbs/books/86/ref=zg_bs_nav_b_1_b

[5] Amazon Charts:
https://www.amazon.com/charts

[6] Amazon Best Sellers from 1995 to present:
https://www.amazon.com/gp/bestsellers/2018/books/ref=zg_bsar_cal_ye

Barnes & Noble:

[7] Barnes & Noble homepage: https://www.barnesandnoble.com

[8] Book Graph:
https://www.barnesandnoble.com/book-graph-recommendations

[9] Discover Categories:
https://www.barnesandnoble.com/b/discover-categories/_/N-2noh

[10] B&N Top 100:
https://www.barnesandnoble.com/b/books/_/N-1fZ29Z8q8

[11] Science & Technology Best Sellers:
https://www.barnesandnoble.com/b/books/science-technolo-gy/_/N-1fZ29Z8q8Z184l

[12]Barnes & Noble Stores' Bestsellers:
https://www.barnesandnoble.com/b/barnes-noble-stores-bestsellers/_/N-1p2x

Other Resources:

[13] Walmart books: https://www.walmart.com/cp/books/3920

[14] Target Books:
https://www.target.com/c/books-movies-music/-/N-5xsxd

[15] Powell's Books: http://www.powells.com

[16] eBay Books: https://www.ebay.com/rpp/books

[17] The New York Times Best Sellers:
https://www.nytimes.com/books/best-sellers

[18] Publishers Weekly: https://www.publishersweekly.com

[19] USA Today Best-selling Books:
https://www.usatoday.com/life/books/best-selling

[20] Los Angeles Times Best Sellers: http://projects.latimes.com/bestsellers

[21] Indie Best Sellers: https://www.indiebound.org/indie-bestsellers

[22] Thriftbooks: https://www.thriftbooks.com

[23] Penguin Random House: https://www.penguinrandomhouse.com

[24] Audible: https://www.audible.com

[25] Hudson Booksellers: https://www.hudsonbooksellers.com

[26] Books-A-Million (BAM): http://www.booksamillion.com

[27] Magazines.com: https://www.magazines.com

[28] Listopia: https://www.goodreads.com/list

[29] "Best of" Lists: https://www.goodreads.com/list/best_by_date

[30] Most Popular Book Lists:
https://www.goodreads.com/list/popular_lists

[31] Book Industry Study Group: http://bisg.org

[32] Complete BISAC Subject Headings: http://bisg.org/page/bisacedition

[33] City of Houston Economy And Trade:
http://www.houstontx.gov/abouthouston/economytrade.html

[34] Wix: https://www.wix.com

[35] Blogger: https://www.blogger.com

[36] Wordpress: https://wordpress.com

[37] Google Analytics: https://analytics.google.com/analytics/web

[38] Adding Your Google Analytics Code to Your Site:
https://support.wix.com/en/article/adding-your-google-analytics-code-to-your-site

[39] Wix Analytics: https://www.wix.com/app-market/category/analytics

[40] Using Analytics with Blogger:
https://support.google.com/blogger/answer/7039627?hl=en

[41] Wordpress stats: https://en.support.wordpress.com/stats

[42] MailChimp: https://mailchimp.com

[43] Understanding landing page experience:
https://support.google.com/adwords/answer/2404197

[44] AdWords advertising policy:
https://support.google.com/adwordspolicy/answer/6008942?hl=en

Chapter II Resources

[1]XMind: http://www.xmind.net

[2] FreeMind: http://freemind.sourceforge.net

[3] Freeplane: https://www.freeplane.org/wiki/index.php/Home

[4] Improve Your Paper by Writing Structured Paragraphs (University of Wisconsin-Madison):
https://writing.wisc.edu/Handbook/Paragraphing.html

[5] Purdue OWL: Paragraphs and Paragraphing:
https://owl.english.purdue.edu/owl/resource/606/01

[6] Paragraph Length: University of Bristol:
http://www.bristol.ac.uk/arts/exercises/grammar/grammar_tutorial/page_39.htm

[7] iTunes Voice Recorder & Audio Editor:
https://itunes.apple.com/us/app/voice-recorder-audio-editor/id685310398?mt=8

[8] Smart Recorder(Android):
https://play.google.com/store/apps/details?id=com.andrwq.recorder&hl=en

[9] Grammarly: https://www.grammarly.com

[10] Upwork Editors: https://www.upwork.com/hire/editors

[11] Evernote: https://evernote.com

[12] Trello: https://trello.com

[13] How to create a table of contents by marking text in word: https://support.microsoft.com/en-us/help/285059/how-to-create-a-table-of-contents-by-marking-text-in-word

Chapter III Resources

[1] Book Trim Sizes and Maximum Page Counts (CreateSpace): https://www.createspace.com/Special/Pop/book_trimsizes-pagecount.html

[2] The Story of the Social Security Number: https://www.ssa.gov/policy/docs/ssb/v69n2/v69n2p55.html

[3] ISBN-13: https://www.isbn.org/faqs_general_questions#isbn_faq16

[4] Bowker: Purchase ISBNs: https://www.myidentifiers.com/Get-your-isbn-now

[5] Amazon Standard Identification Numbers (ASINs): https://www.amazon.com/gp/seller/asin-upc-isbn-info.html

[6] CreateSpace-Assigned ISBN: https://www.createspace.com/Products/Book/ISBNs.jsp

[7] MyIdentifiers: https://www.myidentifiers.com

[8] Barcodes: http://www.bowker.com/products/Barcode.html

[9] Buy Barcodes: https://www.myidentifiers.com/barcode/main#click_to_buy_barcode

[10] Printing and Scanning Fees: https://www.createspace.com/Special/Enterprise/Publisher/printing_scanning_fees.jsp

[11] Supported eBook Formats:
https://kdp.amazon.com/en_US/help/topic/G200634390

[12] International Publishers Association Endorses EPUB 3 as Global Standard: http://idpf.org/ipa_endorses_epub_3

[13] Calibre: https://calibre-ebook.com/download

[14] Adobe InDesign:
https://www.adobe.com/products/indesign.html

[15] Adobe InDesign Experts:
https://www.upwork.com/hire/adobe-indesign-experts

[16] Interior Templates:
https://forums.createspace.com/en/community/docs/DOC-1323

[17] Book Cover Design freelancers:
https://www.upwork.com/hire/book-cover-design-freelancers

[18] CreateSpace Artwork Templates:
https://www.createspace.com/Help/Book/Artwork.do

[19] CreateSpace submission guidelines:
https://www.createspace.com/Special/Enterprise/Publisher/submission_guidelines.jsp

[20] Create an eBook Cover:
https://kdp.amazon.com/en_US/help/topic/G200645690

Chapter IV Resources

[1]KDP Jumpstart:
https://kdp.amazon.com/en_US/help/topic/G202187740

[2] List Price Requirements:
https://kdp.amazon.com/en_US/help/topic/G200634560

[3] Reduce Your eBook Manuscript File Size:
https://kdp.amazon.com/en_US/help/topic/G200730380

[4] eBook Royalty Options:
https://kdp.amazon.com/en_US/help/topic/G200644210

[5] Linking eBook and Paperback Editions:
https://kdp.amazon.com/en_US/help/topic/G200652220

[6] Smashwords Distribution Information Page:
https://www.smashwords.com/distribution

[7] Smashwords Style Guide:
https://www.smashwords.com/books/view/52

[8] IDPF EPUB Validator: http://validator.idpf.org

[9] Smashwords Support Center FAQ:
https://www.smashwords.com/about/supportfaq

[10] You Should Take Kindle's Last Rivalry Seriously:
https://www.wired.com/2015/04/kobo-new-ereader

[11] Kobo eReader Store: https://us.kobobooks.com/pages/retailers

[12] Kobo Writing Life - Frequently Asked Questions:
http://download.kobobooks.com/writinglife/Kobo/en-US/KWL_FAQ.pdf

[13] Kobo Writing Life Independent Publishers Program Terms & Conditions:
https://merch.kobobooks.com/writinglife/en-US/serviceAgreement.html

[14] Kobo Writing Life: https://www.kobo.com/us/en/p/writinglife

[15] CreateSpace Homepage: https://www.createspace.com

[16] CreateSpace Book Royalty:
https://www.createspace.com/Products/Book

[17] Expanded Distribution:
https://www.createspace.com/Products/Book/ExpandedDistribution.jsp

[18] Create Your Account with IngramSpark:
https://myaccount.ingramspark.com/Account/Signup

[19] Create Your Account with Lightning Source: https://myaccount.lightningsource.com/account/signup

[20] How much will my printed book cost? http://connect.lulu.com/en/discussion/33671

[21] Lulu homepage: https://www.lulu.com

[22] Sell & Distribute Page (Blurb): http://www.blurb.com/sell-and-distribute

[23] IngramSpark features: http://www.ingramspark.com/features

[24] Market Access Fee: https://help.lightningsource.com/hc/en-us/articles/210276566-Market-Access-Fee

[25] How to Submit File Revisions: https://help.ingramspark.com/hc/en-us/articles/209072506-How-to-Submit-File-Revisions

[26] File Requirements for Print Books: http://www.ingramspark.com/blog/file-requirements-for-print-books

[27] How to Create E-Book Files for IngramSpark: http://www.ingramspark.com/plan-your-book/ebooks/epub-guidelines

[28] IngramSpark Publisher Compensation Calculator. https://myaccount.ingramspark.com/Portal/Tools/PubCompCalculator

Chapter V Resources

[1] Amazon Marketing Service Sponsored Products and Product Display Ads: https://images-na.ssl-images-amazon.com/images/G/01/AdProductsWebsite/downloads/AMS_Book_Ads_FAQ.pdf

[2] Amazon Marketing Services Agreement: https://ams.amazon.com/terms

[3] Sponsored Products: How to Get Started Tutorial: https://www.youtube.com/watch?v=LgWM97W6dt4

[4] Amazon Marketing Services 101: Getting Started with Product Display Ads: https://www.youtube.com/watch?v=ri3W8cycGSA

[5] Advertising for KDP eBooks: https://kdp.amazon.com/en_US/help/topic/G201499010

[6] KDP Select: https://kdp.amazon.com/en_US/select

[7] Kindle Unlimited: https://www.amazon.com/gp/feature.html?docId=1002872331

[8] Kindles Owners' Lending Library (KOLL): https://www.amazon.com/gp/help/customer/display.html?nodeId=200757120

[9] Adding a Kindle Countdown Deal: https://kdp.amazon.com/en_US/help/topic/G201298280

[10] Featured Kindle Countdown Deals: https://www.amazon.com/Kindle-eBooks/b?ie=UTF8&node=7078878011

[11] Free Book Promotions: https://kdp.amazon.com/en_US/help/topic/G201298240

[12] Sales Ranking: https://kdp.amazon.com/en_US/help/topic/G201648140

[13] Kindle Reader app: https://www.amazon.com/kindle-dbs/fd/kcp

[14] Purchase a Kindle Book as a Gift: https://www.amazon.com/gp/help/customer/display.html?nodeId=201964280

[15] Kindle eBook Pre-order: https://kdp.amazon.com/en_US/help/topic/G201499380

[16] KDP Jumpstart Topic 3 - Write Your Book Description: https://kdp.amazon.com/en_US/help/topic/G202187790

[17] Supported HTML for Book Description: https://kdp.amazon.com/en_US/help/topic/G201189630

Chapter VI Resources:

[1] Managing Editorial Reviews:
https://authorcentral.amazon.com/gp/help?topicID=200649600

[2] What is Amazon Vine? https://www.amazon.com/gp/vine/help

[3] What is Advantage?
https://www.amazon.com/gp/seller-account/mm-product-page.html?topic=200329780

[4] Amazon's Top Customer Reviewers:
https://www.amazon.com/review/top-reviewers

[5] Hall of Fame Reviewers:
https://www.amazon.com/hz/leaderboard/hall-of-fame

[6] About Amazon Verified Purchase Reviews:
https://www.amazon.com/gp/help/customer/display.html/ref=hp_20079100_verifiedreviews?nodeId=201145140

[7] About Customer Reviews:
https://www.amazon.com/gp/help/customer/display.html/ref=hp_left_v4_sib?ie=UTF8&nodeId=201967050

[8] Community Guidelines:
https://www.amazon.com/gp/help/customer/display.html?nodeId=201929730

[9] Customer Reviews Guidelines Frequently Asked Questions from Authors:
https://www.amazon.com/gp/community-help/customer-review-guidelines-faqs-from-authors

[10] Send & receive private messages:
https://support.google.com/youtube/answer/57955?hl=en

[11] Goodreads Introduces Kindle Ebook Giveaways Beta Program (U.S. market):
https://www.goodreads.com/blog/show/646-goodreads-introduces-kindle-ebook-giveaways-beta-program-u-s-market

[12] Giveaways: https://www.goodreads.com/giveaway

[13] Giveaway Terms & Conditions:
https://www.goodreads.com/giveaway/terms

[14] Walt Disney's signature:
https://en.wikipedia.org/wiki/Walt_Disney#/media/File:Walt_Disney_1942_signature.svg

[15] Goodreads Groups: https://www.goodreads.com/group

[16] How do I add friends? (Goodreads):
https://www.goodreads.com/help/show/13-how-do-i-add-friends

[17] Advertise with Goodreads: https://www.goodreads.com/advertisers

[18] Add an event (Goodreads):
https://www.goodreads.com/help/show/240-how-do-i-add-an-event-to-my-author-profile

[19] Goodreads Review Programs:
https://www.goodreads.com/about/review_program

[20] The Goodreads Author Program:
https://www.goodreads.com/author/program

[21] Signup LinkedIn: https://www.linkedin.com/start/join

[22] Inviting or Connecting with People on LinkedIn:
https://www.linkedin.com/help/linkedin/answer/118/inviting-or-connecting-with-people-on-linkedin?lang=en

[23] "Like" and "Unlike" Shared Content or Comments:
https://www.linkedin.com/help/linkedin/answer/3751/-like-and-unlike-shared-content-or-comments?lang=en

[24] Commenting on Posts and Comments (LinkedIn):
https://www.linkedin.com/help/linkedin/answer/3068/commenting-on-posts-and-comments?lang=en

[25] Finding and Joining a Group (LinkedIn): https://www.linkedin.com/help/linkedin/answer/186/finding-and-joining-a-group?lang=en

[26] Sharing Content on LinkedIn:
https://www.linkedin.com/help/linkedin/answer/84813/sharing-content-on-linkedin-best-practices?lang=en

[27] Twitter search engine: https://twitter.com/search-home

[28] Advanced search: https://twitter.com/search-advanced

[29] About different types of Tweets:
https://help.twitter.com/en/using-twitter/types-of-tweets

[30] Frequently Asked Questions: https://www.reddit.com/wiki/faq

[31] Redditquette: https://www.reddit.com/wiki/reddiquette

[32] Create an account in Reddit: https://www.reddit.com/register

[33] Reddit internal search engine:
https://www.reddit.com/subreddits/search

[34] Classic Cars (subreddit): https://www.reddit.com/r/classiccars

[35] Muscle Car (subreddit) https://www.reddit.com/r/musclecar

Chapter VII: Resources

[1] Consideration for Product Listing on BN.com and Retail Store Placement:
https://help.barnesandnoble.com/app/answers/detail/a_id/2155

[2] CreateSpace Titles on BN.com:
https://help.barnesandnoble.com/app/answers/detail/a_id/3552

[3] Powell's Books: http://www.powells.com

[4] Small Press Publishers. Interested in Listing Your Books with Powell's Books?
http://www.powells.com/info/publisher-info

[5] Google Sheets: https://www.google.com/sheets/about

[6] Burton Barr Central Library: http://www.phoenixpubliclibrary.org

[7] Homepage of Meetup.com: https://www.meetup.com

[8] Meetups in San Francisco:
https://www.meetup.com/cities/us/ca/san_francisco

[9] Build a leadership team:
https://www.meetup.com/help/article/868703/

[10] Leilas Hair Museum - Hair Jewelries: http://leilashairmuseum.net

[11] Museum of Bad Art: http://www.museumofbadart.org

[12] Raumen Museum: http://www.raumen.co.jp/english

[13] Eventbrite Homepage: https://www.eventbrite.com

[14] Eventbrite Help Center: https://www.eventbrite.com/support

[15] How to create an event:
https://www.eventbrite.com/support/articles/en_US/Multi_Group_
How_To/how-to-create-an-event?lg=en_US

[16] Find the package that's right for you:
https://www.eventbrite.com/organizer/pricing

[17] Eventbrite Essentials:
https://www.eventbrite.com/organizer/essentials

[18] Eventbrite Professional:
https://www.eventbrite.com/organizer/professional

[19] How to change your Eventbrite package:
https://www.eventbrite.com/support/articles/en_US/Multi_Group_
How_To/how-to-change-your-eventbrite-package?lg=en_US

[20] Eventbrite Payment Processing (EPP):
https://www.eventbrite.com/support/articles/en_US/Troubleshooting/
getting-started-with-eventbrite-payment-processing?lg=en_US

[21] What features are unavailable with PayPal and Authorize.net?
https://www.eventbrite.com/support/articles/en_US/How_To/what-fea-
tures-are-unavailable-with-paypal-and-authorize-net?lg=en_US

[22] How to accept payments by check, invoice, or at the event with offline payments:
https://www.eventbrite.com/support/articles/en_US/How_To/how-to-accept-payments-by-check-invoice-or-at-the-event-with-offline-payments?lg=en_US

[23] How to set up event payout details:
https://www.eventbrite.com/support/articles/en_US/How_To/how-to-set-up-event-payout-details?lg=en_US

[24] How To Design a Great Event Page (It's Better Than Using Azul!):
https://www.eventbrite.com/blog/ds00-how-to-design-a-great-event-page-its-better-than-using-azul

[25] Getting started with Eventbrite invitations and email communication:
https://www.eventbrite.com/support/articles/en_US/Troubleshooting/getting-started-with-eventbrite-invitations-and-email-communication?lg=en_US

[26] CAN-SPAM Act: A Compliance Guide for Business:
https://www.ftc.gov/tips-advice/business-center/guidance/can-spam-act-compliance-guide-business

[27] How to create and send email invitations for your event:
https://www.eventbrite.com/support/articles/en_US/Multi_Group_How_To/how-to-create-and-send-email-invitations-for-your-event?lg=en_US

[28] Eventbrite Spectrum: https://www.eventbrite.com/spectrum

[29] How to increase ticket sales with an affiliate program:
https://www.eventbrite.com/support/articles/en_US/Multi_Group_How_To/how-to-increase-ticket-sales-with-an-affiliate-program?lg=en_US

[30] Promoted Listings Extension:
https://www.eventbrite.com/spectrum/promoted-listings

[31] How to set up Eventbrite's Promoted Listings to reach more people:
https://www.eventbrite.com/support/articles/en_US/How_To/how-to-set-up-eventbrite-s-promoted-listings-to-reach-more-people?lg=en_US

[32] How to manage and optimize your Promoted Listings campaigns: https://www.eventbrite.com/support/articles/en_US/Troubleshooting/how-to-manage-and-optimize-your-promoted-listings-campaigns?lg=en_US

[33] Promoted Listings Emails: https://s3.amazonaws.com/eventbrite-s3/marketing/landingpages/assets/pdfs/Promoted+Listings+Pricing+and+City+List.pdf

[34] Advertise Your Event in Eventbrite's Attendee Emails: https://docs.google.com/forms/d/e/1FAIpQLScGqdr36No_six6yvoiT-WjvfHFOtbZ7vXYOMZx87-JtkOjvMA/viewform

[35] How to set up discount codes for one or multiple events: https://www.eventbrite.com/support/articles/en_US/How_To/how-to-set-up-discount-codes-for-one-or-multiple-events?lg=en_US

[36] How to set up access codes for hidden tickets for one or multiple events: https://www.eventbrite.com/support/articles/en_US/How_To/how-to-set-up-access-codes-for-hidden-tickets-for-one-or-multiple-events?lg=en_US

[37] How to add your Eventbrite event to Facebook and sell tickets: https://www.eventbrite.com/support/articles/en_US/How_To/how-to-publish-your-eventbrite-event-to-facebook-and-sell-tickets?lg=en_US

[38] Bitly: URL Shortener and Link Management Platform: https://bitly.com

[39] Google URL Shortener: https://goo.gl

[40] Google Sheets: https://docs.google.com/spreadsheets

[41] Google Voice: https://www.google.com/voice

[42] Skype: https://www.skype.com

Skype Coaching Program

Using coaching services to help you self-publish your book may seem counterproductive considering you have a treasure chest of information right in front of you. If you're a motivated person with a strong grasp of the strategies taught in this guide, then you're right; my coaching services most likely won't be of use to you. However, if you feel like you have a decent understanding of the bits-and-pieces of how self-publishing works, but you still feel like "it's something you're missing" that's stopping you from bringing your idea into fruition, then my coaching services may be the catalyst needed to get you over the hump.

There are many decisions to make as a self-publisher, such as which print-on-demand services to use and what trim size is most appropriate for your book. All of these choices can be stressful and could lead to analysis paralysis. That's why it's a good idea to consult a domain expert who has been deep-in-the-trenches and understands what it takes to reach self-publishing success. We all reach stumbling blocks in life sooner or later, and having someone who can help set you on the right trajectory is valuable.

Here are several key reasons why self-publishing coaching may be right for you:

You get customized solutions: We all have unique routes along the self-publishing highway. Perhaps it's a lack of confidence that's keeping you from writing the first words, or maybe you're not sure if your situation requires you to register an ISBN. Getting a one-on-one talk means that your burning questions get answered and that the road will be clear for you to drive towards self-publishing happiness.

High-quality feedback: Your manuscript or book idea will be analyzed. Constructive criticism will be given to serve as a compass for your self-publishing success. Book publishing is a business, and it's always a good idea to ensure your book is viable and meets world-class standards. A high-quality book will open the doors to further promotional opportunities.

You need an accountability partner: If you had an idea for a book brewing in your head for years, or possibly decades, then now is the time to put those thoughts into motion. If you need someone to help you break your writing duties into more manageable chunks so that you will make steady and predictable progress, then coaching may be right for you. There's a lot to get done: research, writing, editing, publishing, and promotion. Having someone to help align your activities with your schedule will do wonders for your productivity.

To learn more about my coaching services visit this URL: http://www.purcellconsult.com/selfpub-coaching

Index

www.ingramcontent.com/pod-product-compliance
Lightning Source LLC
LaVergne TN
LVHW011404080426
835511LV00005B/408